Catalyst 5.8

The Perl MVC Framework

Build scalable and extendable web applications using
the Agile MVC framework

Antano Solar John

Catalyst 5.8
The Perl MVC Framework

First published: June 2010

Production Reference: 1220610

Published by Packt Publishing Ltd.
32 Lincoln Road
Olton
Birmingham, B27 6PA, UK.

ISBN 978-1-847199-24-9

www.packtpub.com

Cover Image by Vinayak Chittar (vinayak.chittar@gmail.com)

Credits

Author

Antano Solar John

Reviewer

Robert Sedlacek

Acquisition Editor

Douglas Paterson

Development Editor

Dhiraj Chandiramani

Technical Editor

Smita Solanki

Indexer

Monica Ajmera Mehta

Editorial Team Leader

Aanchal Kumar

Project Team Leader

Priya Mukherji

Project Coordinator

Leena Purkait

Proofreader

Lynda Sliwoski

Graphics

Geetanjali Sawant

Production Coordinator

Aparna S. Bhagat

Cover Work

Aparna S. Bhagat

About the Author

Antano Solar John is a tech evangelist who is passionate about using technology to revolutionize the learning experience! He authored his first book on MODx with Packt in 2008 which was also the first book ever written on this platform.

Antano has contributed massively to the open source community in terms of documentation, code, and support on various platforms based on PHP, Perl, Lisp, Python, Ruby, and so on. His contribution to the open source world has allowed him to meet and model from a variety of people who have learned to code and think naturally! His writing skills benefit from this advantage thereby bringing structure and clarity to the learner.

Antano's first technical publication titled "Help AI Help You-Swiss Knife of Communication" was on Communication and Machine Learning using Neuro Linguistic Programming (NLP) concepts such as Meta Modelling and Deep Structures, which was critically acclaimed by communication and technology experts. He has also been recently certified as a licensed NLP practitioner by its cofounder Richard Bandler. Other papers by Antano include "802.11 MAC Enhancements-Breaking Barriers of Wireless Speed" that was published in the IEEE Journal, "Learning to Develop in the Open Source World", and so on.

Owing to his experience as a consultant and trainer, Antano has designed course structure and content for corporate learners at different levels on subjects such as Object Oriented Perl, Unix System Fundamentals, Shell basic, Ruby on Rails, and so on. In association with MaFoi Ranstad, Antano entirely designed and implemented a structured course for transitioning web designers into developers through a one-day blended learning program called "Learn".

Antano has been keenly focusing on Accelerated Learning. He has conducted workshops at various reputed colleges and corporate events on how to learn quickly and effectively-technology languages and platforms using strategies that he has developed. His experience with NLP, which is the science of Modelling Excellence has helped him with this effort.

As part of his consultant assignments he has worked on Catalyst from its early stages. He has been a consultant and a trainer providing IT solutions and sessions on VoIP, networks, and software platforms, and languages. Currently, he is the Chief Technology Officer (CTO) at NuVeda Learning. In his present role, he is responsible for accelerated learning solutions which leverages technology for speed and scale.

Antano's other interests include Music, Dance, Martial Arts, and Chess. He used to play Chess professionally as a child. Antano used to run a successful gaming business when gaming as a business was almost unheard of. He has also won the yahoo hack award twice in India consequently, once for developing a Collaborative Browsing Mechanism using lines of code shorter than this biography without any server or proxy and then yet again for developing a Hybrid Search Engine from scratch in 24 hours that uses Machine and Social Intelligence to identify, search, and distill information in contexts you expect!

I first like to thank the Catalyst Community without whom this book could have never been possible. I also convey my gratitude to the original author Jonathan, other members of the community like Matt S. Trout, Jess Robinson along with all those who taught me Catalyst!

Special appreciation to the reviewer Robert Sedlacek and the Packt team (Leena Purkait , Dhiraj Chandiramani, and Smita Solanki) for continually providing valuable inputs to improve the reading experience.

About the Reviewer

Robert Sedlacek started programming at the age of 17 while working as computer hardware technician. He started out with Perl, took a four-year break into other platforms and has been developing in Perl ever since. Today he is working as a general Perl contractor but also specializes in web application development with Catalyst.

Table of Contents

Preface

Have you ever created a web application that is almost done but is hard to complete? It is a well known fact that 20 percent of the work takes 80 percent of the time in software development (80-20 rule Frednic Brooks). One of the reasons contributing to this is that it is easy to build web applications, but it's not so easy to build clean, scalable, and extendable web applications. MVC architecture aims at reducing most of the overheads involved in making this transition easy. Catalyst provides a mechanism to implement MVC and more complex design patterns for web application development. This books aims at taking you step- by-step from showing how MVC simplifies creating quality applications to how Catayst allows you to tap this power instantly. The book then takes the journey of good practices and continues to decouple the abstracted layers to explain how to use any object of your choice. The book finally explains advanced design patterns and concludes with the improvements that MOOSE brings in to all this.

What this book covers

Chapter 1, Introduction to Catalyst serves as an introduction to Catalyst and its features. You will also learn how to install it and get it up and running.

Chapter 2, Creating a Catalyst Application shows how to create a Catalyst application skeleton, step through the different files in its directories, and learn how to generate HTML output and connect a SQLite database to Catalyst.

Chapter 3, Building a Real Application covers the building of our first real application—the address book. We learn to design and apply the "CRUD" interface to the database of our site and write some Catalyst actions.

Chapter 4, Expanding the Application explains how to make deployment easy by using the configuration file. We add some of the most common features that web applications need to our address book application. We learn how to add sessions to our application programmed search logic and to identify users and use their identity to control access to the application. We will also learn how to display resultsets that span multiple pages. Finally, we will learn how to utilize our application's model outside of our application. Later, we explore authentication and authorization by implementing page-level and record-level access control.

Chapter 5, Building a More Advanced Application covers how to build a new application called ChatStat. Here we explore the features of DBIC for easy handling of data and use Catalyst to get the data from DBIC onto the Web.

Chapter 6, Building Your Own Model covers the different ways to access the data model. We learn to write a database model and create a filesystem model from scratch, which is integrated with the Catalyst application.

Chapter 7, Hot Web Topics covers the development of a REST API to give the user easy access to our application's data. We also learn to add AJAX interactivity and incorporate RSS feeds in our application.

Chapter 8, Moose shows how Moose can make declarations of methods and properties simpler in our application. We also examine how chained controllers can be easily defined with Catalyst::Declare. We will also discover how Moose allows for Method Signatures and Property constraints along with best practices.

Chapter 9, Deployment teaches us to package our application and make it available as a PAR file, ready to run on a real web server.

Chapter 10, Testing covers an important part of any project, that is, testing. We learn to write programs to test our Catalyst application automatically. We see how to test the individual non-Catalyst components, and then the components inside Catalyst.

What you need for this book

A working machine using Linux, OS X, or Windows on which you have permission to install Perl and Perl packages.

Who this book is for

This book is written for Perl developers who want to start or strengthen their skill and understanding of web application development using MVC principles.

Conventions

In this book, you will find a number of styles of text that distinguish between different kinds of information. Here are some examples of these styles, and an explanation of their meaning.

Code words in text are shown as follows: "The next step is to create a template in the root/hello directory."

A block of code is set as follows:

```
sub atom : Local {
  my ($self, $c) = @_;
  $c->stash->{type} = 'Atom';
}
```

When we wish to draw your attention to a particular part of a code block, the relevant lines or items are set in bold:

```
package AddressBook::Controller::Address;
use Moose;
use namespace::autoclean;
BEGIN {extends 'Catalyst::Controller'; }
extends 'Catalyst::Controller::FormBuilder';
=head1 NAME
```

Any command-line input or output is written as follows:

```
$ apt-get install libcatalyst-perl
```

New terms and **important words** are shown in bold. Words that you see on the screen, in menus or dialog boxes for example, appear in the text like this: "The first link on the index page is **Look at all people**."

Warnings or important notes appear in a box like this.

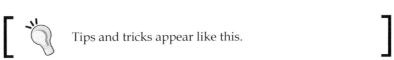

Tips and tricks appear like this.

Reader feedback

Feedback from our readers is always welcome. Let us know what you think about this book—what you liked or may have disliked. Reader feedback is important for us to develop titles that you really get the most out of.

To send us general feedback, simply send an email to feedback@packtpub.com, and mention the book title via the subject of your message.

If there is a book that you need and would like to see us publish, please send us a note in the **SUGGEST A TITLE** form on www.packtpub.com or email suggest@packtpub.com.

If there is a topic that you have expertise in and you are interested in either writing or contributing to a book on, see our author guide on www.packtpub.com/authors.

Customer support

Now that you are the proud owner of a Packt book, we have a number of things to help you to get the most from your purchase.

Downloading the example code for the book

You can download the example code files for all Packt books you have purchased from your account at http://www.PacktPub.com. If you purchased this book elsewhere, you can visit http://www.PacktPub.com/support and register to have the files e-mailed directly to you.

Errata

Although we have taken every care to ensure the accuracy of our content, mistakes do happen. If you find a mistake in one of our books—maybe a mistake in the text or the code—we would be grateful if you would report this to us. By doing so, you can save other readers from frustration, and help us to improve subsequent versions of this book. If you find any errata, please report them by visiting http://www.packtpub.com/support, selecting your book, clicking on the **let us know** link, and entering the details of your errata. Once your errata are verified, your submission will be accepted and the errata added to any list of existing errata. Any existing errata can be viewed by selecting your title from http://www.packtpub.com/support.

Piracy

Piracy of copyright material on the Internet is an ongoing problem across all media. At Packt, we take the protection of our copyright and licenses very seriously. If you come across any illegal copies of our works, in any form, on the Internet, please provide us with the location address or website name immediately so that we can pursue a remedy.

Please contact us at copyright@packtpub.com with a link to the suspected pirated material.

We appreciate your help in protecting our authors, and our ability to bring you valuable content.

Questions

You can contact us at questions@packtpub.com if you are having a problem with any aspect of the book, and we will do our best to address it.

1
Introduction to Catalyst

Writing a web application is usually a repetitive process. For every page, you create a new script. This script performs essentially the same tasks as the other scripts in the application such as connecting to a database, getting some input from the user, and producing a web page as the result. This style of application design results in a structure, as shown in the following screenshot:

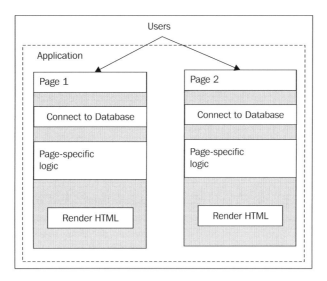

It may be useful to note that this concerns traditional non-framework designs, as there are more web frameworks for Perl.

Building an application with this sort of design is certainly not a difficult process, but the constant repetition can be prone to error. If you decide to change your database, you will have to update the database connection string in each file. If you happen to forget one obscure file, you might not be aware until your users start sending you angry e-mails.

Of course, this problem is not limited to the database connection strings. As the next diagram shows, repeated elements are there everywhere. As each page generates its own HTML, a request from your web designer to update the layout of a page will involve having to dig through your Perl source code (potentially breaking database queries or other logic), just to change some HTML. In addition, whenever you make a change that affects your entire site or application, you'll have to make the change a number of times—once for each page. Similarly, fixing one bug will entail copying the fix to every other place. This is inconvenient, a waste of time, and just plain boring.

Catalyst is an open source Perl-based **Model-View-Controller** (**MVC**) framework that aims to solve this problem by reorganizing your web application.

Catalyst application architecture

Rather than making each location that a user may visit as an individual file, we make each location an action inside a `Controller` class. Catalyst sits in front of each of these Controllers, and when it receives a request, it dispatches the request to the proper action. When an action is called by the dispatcher, it's in a preconfigured environment—all configuration options have been read from a configuration file at the application start, all databases are connected, all parameters from the request have been parsed, and so on. All your action has to do is implement the logic associated with the request; there is no setup that you have to manually perform, as illustrated in the following diagram:

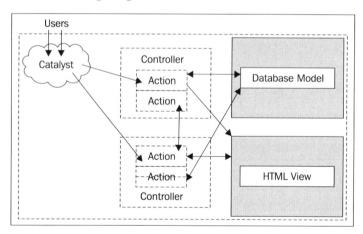

Although this dispatch mechanism is already an improvement over the traditional process, Catalyst doesn't stop here. Your actions can call on the help of Models and Views as well.

In fact, for more complex problem domains that have a small and flexible Controller handling the actual business logic via models usually gives the most maintainable results.

A Model is a source of data. Most applications use a single relational database such as MySQL or PostgreSQL as their Model, but Catalyst does not require that—you can use anything from files on a disk, to an e-mail server, or remote RSS feeds; also you can have as many Models as your application needs.

Each Model knows how to configure itself at startup (for example, connect to the database server), so you'll never have to worry about that. If you need to use a different database, you can change the connection information in one file, restart your application, and the change will take effect everywhere, automatically. The repetition that a traditional application would require is simply non-existent in Catalyst.

Lastly, a View is another component that your action may use. Only a very limited subset of applications will not need at least one View component.

A View is a way to turn the raw data that your action generates into something more useful to your application's users. Typically, applications have a View that converts the data into an HTML page via a templating system, such as the Template Toolkit, Mason, or ClearSilver.

The View is generally responsible for all matters of representing the response. This also includes serializations such as JSON, or RSS, and Atom feeds.

Templating systems abstract your HTML or XML away from your Perl code, so the web designer can edit it without knowing anything about Perl or the underlying design of your application.

You don't have to completely understand what MVC is right now—we'll start learning the details in the next chapter. For now, think about all the code you've cut and pasted between files in your application and how Catalyst will eliminate that forever.

Extensibility

MVC isn't all that Catalyst provides. At the time of writing, there were over 190 freely available plugins that added new features to Catalyst. Existing plugins offer functionality such as configuration file parsers, specialized logging tools, e-mail interfaces, caching, user authentication and authorization, cryptography, internationalization and localization, browser detection, and even virus scanning. Most of these plugins drop right into your application and instantly provide you with the advertised functionality. This saves you from having to reinvent the wheel for common (and uncommon) tasks.

In addition to plugins, pre-made Models, Controllers, and Views (collectively called components) are also available. As Catalyst is fully object oriented, your application-specific components can simply "subclass" these off-the-shelf components and customize the functionality to whatever degree is necessary.

As new versions of Catalyst are using a powerful system for object orientation called **Moose**, many extensions to components are behaviors that can be composed in, allowing even more flexibility.

Finally, if there's no pre-built component available, there's the possibility that a generic Perl module from the **Comprehensive Perl Archive Network (CPAN)**, which is available at `http://search.cpan.org/`, can help you — there are over 10,000 modules currently available!

Reusability

Another advantage of Catalyst's MVC design is that the components need not be specific to one application. If you're developing a number of related applications, you can share components between them with minimal (or no) modification, as the components are just Perl objects that need not know anything specific about your application. Of course, if you need a component that's specific to your application, that's no problem for Catalyst.

Flexibility

As Catalyst handles all the details of loading your components and handling requests, you aren't tied to any details of this process. This means that you can deploy your application with any web server (Apache and lighttpd are widely used) under whatever configuration best suits your environment. If you're using mod_perl with Apache 1.3, that's no problem for Catalyst. If you're using lighttpd as a proxy to several backend FastCGI servers, Catalyst will work great. Catalyst even comes with a built-in HTTP server, so you can develop applications without having to install and configure a web server.

With Catalyst, like Perl itself, **There Is More Than One Way To Do It** (**TIMTOWTDI**), and Catalyst will bend to fit your environment so you can use what you're already familiar with.

Reliability

Finally, Catalyst is designed to be reliable. The runtime package comes with over 2,600 unit tests that automatically check the reliability of Catalyst when you install it. In the unlikely event that there's something wrong with your Perl environment, Catalyst won't get installed until it's fixed. There's always the possibility of a bug in Catalyst, but nothing major has come up because the core developer team tries to keep Catalyst as small as possible. Everything that's non-essential is kept in plugins or in reusable base components.

This reliability isn't just for the Catalyst developers though. When you create your application (or components within it), unit tests are automatically generated. These tests serve to make sure that your application is at least minimally functional. If you choose to, you can easily add your own automatic tests that can test every part of your application. Rather than manually going through your site when you make a major (or minor) change, you can have the computer double-check everything while you get a cup of coffee. Testing is examined in detail in Chapter 8.

Installing Catalyst

Now that you're convinced that you want to try Catalyst, you just have to install it. As Catalyst is Perl-based, you'll need to have a working version of Perl. Most Linux and BSD distributions come with a suitable Perl in the default install, as do many commercial Unix variants (Mac OS X is no exception). Microsoft Windows doesn't ship with Perl, but you can get a Perl distribution for free from ActiveState, Strawberry Perl, or Cygwin. Regardless of your operating system, you'll need Perl version 5.8.1 or higher (5.8.8, which is the latest at the time of writing, is the version used in this book).

 Version 5.10.x is already out, but as 5.8 is more widely used, the examples should stay that way. Ubuntu, for example, already ships 5.10 for a while.

The easiest way to install Catalyst is via your operating system's package manager. This mostly applies to Linux and the BSDs and the syntax is specific to your distribution. On Debian-based versions of GNU/Linux, the command is:

```
$ apt-get install libcatalyst-perl
```

On FreeBSD or OpenBSD, you can build the Catalyst port by running the following commands as root:

```
$ cd /usr/ports/www/p5-Catalyst-Runtime
$ make install
```

If you're using ActiveState on Windows, ActiveState has a **PPM (Perl Package Manager)** package for Catalyst. You can find the PPM at `http://cpan.uwinnipeg.ca/dist/ Catalyst-Runtime`.

Finally, be sure to check your operating system's manual for specific instructions on installing packages. The latest details are available from the Catalyst installation guide at `http://search.cpan.org/perldoc?Catalyst::Manual::Installation`.

CPAN

If your operating system doesn't provide packages, installing Catalyst directly from the **CPAN** is a simple process. Perl ships with a utility called `cpan` that handles the installation process for you. Simply run the following from the command line:

```
$ cpan Catalyst::Runtime Catalyst::Devel
```

and Catalyst (and all of its dependencies) will be downloaded, integrity-checked, and installed.

The disadvantage of this approach is that you'll need a C compiler `gcc`, `make`, and related development utilities. Most Linux distributions have these available, but they aren't a part of the default install. Mac OS X offers `gcc` and `make` as part of its developer tools package, which you'll need to install if you choose to use `cpan`.

Unfortunately, the `cpan` script is notorious for asking difficult questions the first time that you run it (in order to build a configuration suitable for your system). If you want to avoid these questions and just get Catalyst installed, try the `cat-install` script at `http://www.shadowcat.co.uk/static/cat-install`. You can download that file, run it with Perl, and Catalyst should be installed when it's finished running.

Testing the installation

To test if the installation was successful, try executing `catalyst.pl` from the command prompt. You should see something similar to the following screenshot:

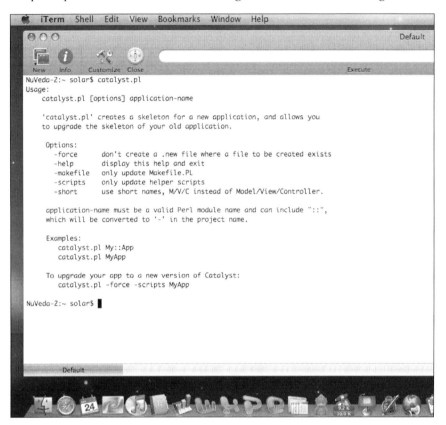

Where to go for help?

If `cpan` is just not working for you and you feel lost, the Catalyst community would love to help you out. The best place for questions is the #catalyst IRC channel at `irc.perl.org`. Users, developers, and other helpful people monitor this channel and are happy to answer Catalyst-related questions.

For longer questions, e-mail is probably a better means of communication. Catalyst has an English-language users list that you can sign up for at `http://lists.scsys.co.uk/cgi-bin/mailman/listinfo/catalyst`.

As Catalyst becomes more popular, new lists are being created for other languages. Catalyst-de was recently created for German-speaking users, and there's interest in creating a Japanese-language mailing list. Many readers of the English list speak other languages, so if you're having trouble with English, say so, and someone can likely assist you in your native language. Catalyst-de still exists but does not really have any traffic anymore. Most of the community and (therefore) the knowledge are now found on the English mailing list.

Finally, the main project website, `http://www.catalystframework.org/`, provides links to useful community tools including the Catalyst wiki, Planet Catalyst (a collection of Catalyst-related blog postings), and the Catalyst Advent Calendar (a mini cookbook published every December).

As always, before posting to the mailing list or asking on IRC, do a quick Google search to see if you're experiencing a common problem.

Summary

Many web applications are implemented in a way that makes developing them painful and repetitive. Catalyst, an MVC framework for Perl, lets you design and implement a web application in a natural, maintainable, and testable manner. Everything that your web application needs to do is written only once. You connect to the database in one place, have configuration in one place, and so on. Then, you just write actions for each URL that your application needs, without worrying about the database connections or HTML to produce. Catalyst will handle the details for you. So, you don't need to worry about writing your applications. Thanks to Catalyst's plugin system, it can do more than just dispatch requests—it can manage sessions and users for you, as well as handle many other common tasks. Catalyst is designed to be reliable. There are hundreds of production applications and thousands of users. The code is well tested and new releases almost always maintain compatibility with applications written for older versions. You don't have to worry about Catalyst breaking your application and slowing down your development. It just works!

Most importantly, Catalyst (and Perl) has a thriving community. You can ask a question on the IRC channel and get a response at almost any time of the day. There are also resources on the web for learning more, blogs from developers and users, recipes on the advent calendar, and a wealth of questions answered on the mailing list.

Although this book does a fairly good job of teaching you how to use Catalyst, to truly be able to continually improve and learn to use Catalyst better, you have to learn from the roots. It is important to realize that Catalyst is just a dispatcher that calls the right ORM, Controller, and View. Each of these is merely Perl modules that are well written. So, to understand the flexibility of Catalyst and to leverage its power, you must understand the various options you have in selecting the Model, View, and Controller methods. In this book, we have outlined a few of the commonly used modules. However, it will be beyond the scope of this book to cover every feature for any of the thought modules. It is merely not possible as these components are continuously being improved. Hence, I recommend that you identify the key Perl module/package being thought/used in each chapter and make the effort to learn it independently outside of Catalyst! For example, `TT`, `DBIx::Class`, and `FormBuider` work with any Perl application. It is important that you understand them that way. Catalyst merely makes your life easier by connecting them for you! So, if I were to have a query on models, I would search for documentation on `DBIx::Class` mostly on `cpan` instead of searching for documents on Catalyst. Template Toolkit has a dedicated site with a guide that takes no longer than 15 minutes to get started with. So does `FormBuilder`. If there is one thing that can make a difference to you from this book, it is this concept that each component that you use in Catalyst has to be learnt and mastered individually outside Catalyst. Even if Catalyst allows you to create an orchestra, you still have to learn the individual instruments—keyboard, violin, and guitar—independently outside the orchestra context.

2

Creating a Catalyst Application

Now that you've installed Catalyst, we are ready to create a simple application. In this chapter, we will be creating a basic application. We'll create the skeleton of the application and write some Catalyst actions (Perl code that gets executed on URL requests). Then we'll learn how to use the **Template Toolkit** (**TT**) to generate HTML output and finally, connect a SQLite database to Catalyst with `DBIx::Class`.

Creating the application skeleton

Catalyst comes with a script called `catalyst.pl` to make this task as simple as possible. `catalyst.pl` takes a single argument, the application's name, and creates an application with that specified name. The name can be any valid Perl module name such as `MyApp` or `MyCompany::HR::Timesheets`.

Let's get started by creating `MyApp`, which is the example application for this chapter:

```
$ catalyst.pl MyApp
created "MyApp"
created "MyApp/script"
created "MyApp/lib"
created "MyApp/root"
created "MyApp/root/static"
created "MyApp/root/static/images"
created "MyApp/t"
created "MyApp/lib/MyApp"
created "MyApp/lib/MyApp/Model"
created "MyApp/lib/MyApp/View"
```

```
created "MyApp/lib/MyApp/Controller"
created "MyApp/myapp.conf"
created "MyApp/lib/MyApp.pm"
created "MyApp/lib/MyApp/Controller/Root.pm"
created "MyApp/README"
created "MyApp/Changes"
created "MyApp/t/01app.t"
created "MyApp/t/02pod.t"
created "MyApp/t/03podcoverage.t"
created "MyApp/root/static/images/catalyst_logo.png"
created "MyApp/root/static/images/btn_120x50_built.png"
created "MyApp/root/static/images/btn_120x50_built_shadow.png"
created "MyApp/root/static/images/btn_120x50_powered.png"
created "MyApp/root/static/images/btn_120x50_powered_shadow.png"
created "MyApp/root/static/images/btn_88x31_built.png"
created "MyApp/root/static/images/btn_88x31_built_shadow.png"
created "MyApp/root/static/images/btn_88x31_powered.png"
created "MyApp/root/static/images/btn_88x31_powered_shadow.png"
created "MyApp/root/favicon.ico"
created "MyApp/Makefile.PL"
created "MyApp/script/myapp_cgi.pl"
created "MyApp/script/myapp_fastcgi.pl"
created "MyApp/script/myapp_server.pl"
created "MyApp/script/myapp_test.pl"
created "MyApp/script/myapp_create.pl"
Change to application directory, and run "perl Makefile.PL" to make sure
your installation is complete.
```

At this point it is a good idea to check if the installation is complete by switching to the newly-created directory (cd MyApp) and running perl Makefile.PL. You should see something like the following:

```
$ perl Makefile.PL
include /Volumes/Home/Users/solar/Projects/CatalystBook/MyApp/inc/Module/
Install.pm
include inc/Module/Install/Metadata.pm
include inc/Module/Install/Base.pm
```

```
Cannot determine perl version info from lib/MyApp.pm
include inc/Module/Install/Catalyst.pm
*** Module::Install::Catalyst
include inc/Module/Install/Makefile.pm
Please run "make catalyst_par" to create the PAR package!
*** Module::Install::Catalyst finished.
include inc/Module/Install/Scripts.pm
include inc/Module/Install/AutoInstall.pm
include inc/Module/Install/Include.pm
include inc/Module/AutoInstall.pm
*** Module::AutoInstall version 1.03
*** Checking for Perl dependencies...
[Core Features]
- Test::More                    ...loaded. (0.94 >= 0.88)
- Catalyst::Runtime             ...loaded. (5.80021 >= 5.80021)
- Catalyst::Plugin::ConfigLoader   ...loaded. (0.23)
- Catalyst::Plugin::Static::Simple ...loaded. (0.29)
- Catalyst::Action::RenderView    ...loaded. (0.14)
- Moose                         ...loaded. (0.99)
- namespace::autoclean          ...loaded. (0.09)
- Config::General               ...loaded. (2.42)
*** Module::AutoInstall configuration finished.
include inc/Module/Install/WriteAll.pm
include inc/Module/Install/Win32.pm
include inc/Module/Install/Can.pm
include inc/Module/Install/Fetch.pm
Writing Makefile for MyApp
Writing META.yml
```

Note that it mentions that all the required modules are available. If any modules are missing, you may have to install those modules using cpan (cpan was explained in *Chapter 1, Introduction to Catalyst*). You can also alternatively install the missing modules by running make followed by make install.

We'll discuss in detail what each of these files do as we progress through the book, but for now, let's just change to the newly-created MyApp directory (cd MyApp) and run the following command:

```
$ perl script/myapp_server.pl
```

This will start up the development web server. You should see some debugging information appear on the console, which is shown as follows:

```
 [debug] Debug messages enabled
[debug] Loaded plugins:
.------------------------------------------------------------------.
| Catalyst::Plugin::ConfigLoader  0.23
| Catalyst::Plugin::Static::Simple  0.21  |
'------------------------------------------------------------------'


[debug] Loaded dispatcher "Catalyst::Dispatcher" [debug] Loaded engine
"Catalyst::Engine::HTTP"
[debug] Found home "/home/jon/projects/book/chapter2/MyApp"
[debug] Loaded Config "/home/jon/projects/book/chapter2/MyApp/myapp.conf"
[debug] Loaded components:
.---------------------------------------------------+----------.
| Class   | Type  +-
----------------------------------------------------+----------+
| MyApp::Controller::Root   |  instance  |
'--------------------------------------  ---------------+----------'


[debug] Loaded Private actions:
.--------------------+-------------- ------------------+--------------.
| Private  | Class  | Method  |
+--------------------+---------------------------------+--------------+
| /default  | MyApp::Controller::Root  | default  |
| /end | MyApp::Controller::Root  | end
|/index  | MyApp::Controller::Root  | index
'--------------------+---------------------------------+--------------'
[debug] Loaded Path actions:
.------------------------------------+------------------------------
----.
| Path                               | Private
|
+------------------------------------+------------------------------
----+
| /                                  | /default
|
```

```
|  /                                    |  /index
|
'---------------------------------------+-------------------------------------
----'
```

```
[info] MyApp powered by Catalyst 5.80004
You can connect to your server at http://localhost:3000
```

This debugging information contains a summary of plugins, Models, Views, and Controllers that your application uses, in addition to showing a map of URLs to actions. As we haven't added anything to the application yet, this isn't particularly helpful, but it will become helpful as we add features.

To see what your application looks like in a browser, simply browse to `http://localhost:3000`. You should see the standard Catalyst welcome page as follows:

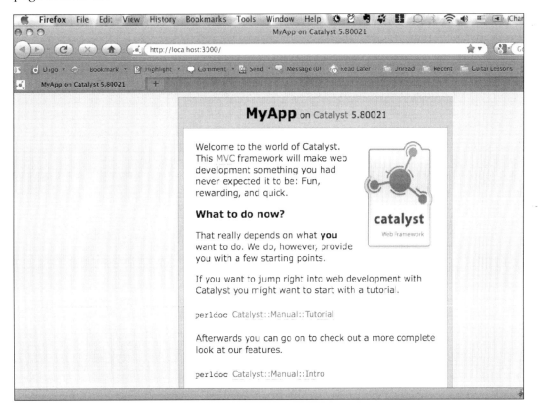

Let's put the application aside for a moment, and see the usage of all the files that were created. The list of files is as shown in the following screenshot:

Before we modify MyApp, let's take a look at how a Catalyst application is structured on a disk. In the root directory of your application, there are some support files. If you're familiar with CPAN modules, you'll be at home with Catalyst. A Catalyst application is structured in exactly the same way (and can be uploaded to the CPAN unmodified, if desired).

This chapter will refer to MyApp as your application's name, so if you use something else, be sure to substitute properly.

Latest helper scripts

Catalyst 5.8 is ported to Moose and the helper scripts for Catalyst were upgraded much later. Therefore, it is necessary for you to check if you have the latest helper scripts. We will discuss helper scripts later. For now, `catalyst.pl` is a helper script and if you're using an updated helper script, then the `lib/MyApp.pm` file (or `lib/whateverappname.pm`) will have the following line:

```
use Moose;
```

If you don't see this line in your application package in the `lib` directory, then you will have to update the helper scripts. You can do that by executing the following command:

```
cpan Catalyst::Helper
```

Files in the MyApp directory

The `MyApp` directory contains the following files:

- `Makefile.PL`: This script generates a `Makefile` to build, test, and install your application. It can also contain a list of your application's CPAN dependencies and automatically install them.

  To run `Makefile.PL` and generate a `Makefile`, simply type `perl Makefile.PL`. After that, you can run `make` to build the application, `make test` to test the application (you can try this right now, as some sample tests have already been created), `make install` to install the application, and so on. For more details, see the `Module::Install` documentation. It's important that you don't delete this file. Catalyst looks for it to determine where the root of your application is.

- `Changes`: This is simply a free-form text file where you can document changes to your application. It's not required, but it can be helpful to end users or other developers working on your application, especially if you're writing an open source application.

- `README`: This is just a text file with information on your application. If you're not going to distribute your application, you don't need to keep it around.

- `myapp.conf`: This is your application's main configuration file, which is loaded when you start your application. You can specify configuration directly inside your application, but this file makes it easier to tweak settings without worrying about breaking your code. `myapp.conf` is in Apache-style syntax, but if you rename the file to `myapp.pl`, you can write it in Perl (or `myapp.yml` for YML format; see the `Config::Any` manual for a complete list).

The name of this file is based on your application's name. Everything is converted to lowercase, double colons are replaced with underscores, and the `.conf` extension is appended.

Files in the lib directory

- The heart of your application lives in the `lib` directory.

- This directory contains a file called `MyApp.pm`. This file defines the namespace and inheritance that are necessary to make this a Catalyst application. It also contains the list of plugins to load application-specific configurations. These configurations can also be defined in the `myapp.conf` file mentioned previously. However, if the same configuration is mentioned in both the files, then the configuration mentioned here takes precedence.

- Inside the `lib` directory, there are three key directories, namely `MyApp/Controller`, `MyApp/Model`, and `MyApp/View`. Catalyst loads the Controllers, Models, and Views from these directories respectively.

Right now, there's one Controller called `Root.pm`. This will handle all root level (/) URLs. This is where the code that generates the welcome page is located.

Keep in mind that `MyApp` is just like any other namespace of a module. The application is created with whatever you passed as an argument to `catalyst.pl` when you created the application. Just like any other module, a namespace with double colons corresponds to subdirectories in the filesystem. For example, `catalyst.pl MyCompany::HR::Timeslips` would create the application with the namespace `MyCompany::HR::Timeslips`. Therefore, it will be represented in the filesystem as `MyCompany/HR/ Timeslips.pm` as the application is created within the `lib` directory when using `catalyst.pl`. The path on the filesystem from the root of your catalyst application will be `lib/MyCompany/HR/ Timeslips.pm`. Similarly, the other files/directories that are created will be `lib/MyCompany/HR/ Timeslips/Controller/`.

Files in the root directory

The next special directory is the `root` directory. This directory will hold your templates and other non-code support files. A subdirectory called `/root/static` is for static content such as images and stylesheets. Catalyst is set up to serve static files from this directory automatically (under the `/static` path), thanks to `Catalyst::Plugin::Static::Simple`. Later, when you deploy your application, you can point your web server at this directory to serve the static files without hitting the application every time.

Files in the script directory

Finally, there is the `script` directory that contains the scripts needed to run, test, and modify your application.

`myapp_server.pl` is the development server; a self-contained HTTP server that you can use to run your application while you're developing it.

`myapp_cgi.pl` is a CGI script for deploying your application with a web server that cannot use **mod_perl** or FastCGI. It's very slow, so use it only as a last resort.

The last server is called `myapp_fastcgi.pl`, which allows you to run your application as a FastCGI server. In Chapter 9, we'll see how to use these scripts to run our application in a production environment.

There are also two utility scripts in this directory. You can use the `myapp_test.pl` script to test an action, without opening a web browser. For example, you can print the source of the welcome page by running the following command line:

```
$ perl script/myapp_test.pl /
```

The last script is `myapp_create.pl`, which is a version of `catalyst.pl` that's customized for your application. It can create Models, Views, Controllers, tests, and many other things. We'll use it in the next two sections to create a View and Model for `MyApp`.

All of the scripts in the `script` directory accept command-line arguments to customize their behavior. `perl script/myapp_<scriptname>.pl --help` will explain the details of that script.

Files in the t directory

The `t` directory is where your application's automatic tests are stored. By default, you'll have the following three tests:

1. `01app.t`, which is a test that passes if your application compiles.
2. `02pod.t`, which will pass if your **Plain Old Documentation** (**POD**) embedded API documentation, inside your application, is *valid*.
3. `03podcoverage.t`, which tests that every public function in your application has some documentation.

You can run the tests in this command by running `make test`, after `Makefile.PL` creates the `Makefile`.

Handling URL requests

When a user makes a request using the browser, Catalyst will look for the appropriate method that can handle the request within packages called Controllers. These Controller methods send back a response to the requesting agent like the browser.

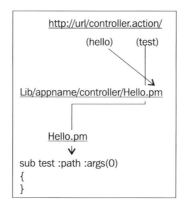

We will discuss in detail later in this chapter how controller methods are mapped to URLs and vice versa. However, for now, let's stick to a basic format where the first argument in the URL is the name of the Controller, the second argument is the method within the Controller, and the rest of the arguments are arguments to the Controller method. For example, `http://localhost:3000/hello/index` will match the `hello` Controller (`Hello.pm`) and `index` will match the subroutine `index` (sub index) within the `hello` Controller (`Hello.pm`).

If the Controller method is not mentioned, then the index method is taken as default.

Let's create a new Controller called "Hello" to check this (this should respond to the `/hello` request):

perl script/myapp_create.pl controller Hello

This will create `/lib/MyApp/Controller/Hello.pm` (and `/t/controller_Hello.t`, which we won't use until Chapter 9). `Hello.pm` will now have the following contents:

```
package MyApp::Controller::Hello;
use Moose;
use namespace::autoclean;
BEGIN {extends 'Catalyst::Controller'; }
=head1 NAME
MyApp::Controller::Hello - Catalyst Controller
```

```
=head1 DESCRIPTION
Catalyst Controller.
=head1 METHODS
=cut
=head2 index
=cut
sub index :Path :Args(0) {
    my ( $self, $c ) = @_;
    $c->response->body('Matched MyApp::Controller::Hello in Hello.');
}
=head1 AUTHOR
  (Your Name on the Machine)
=head1 LICENSE
This library is free software. You can redistribute it and/or modify
it under the same terms as Perl itself.
=cut
__PACKAGE__->meta->make_immutable;

1;
```

This file consists of three parts. At the top is the package declaration (so Perl knows what this module is named), and then some `use` statements (to tell Perl that this module uses Moose). Then, `BEGIN {extends 'Catalyst::Controller'; }` to tell Moose/Perl that this module is a Catalyst Controller. Next, there is some POD (the text starting with =) that you can fill in to provide some API documentation (see `man perlpod` for the syntax). If you don't think you need documentation, you can delete it; it's ignored by Perl. However, it is a good practice to include at least basic documentation for every module and method. The `perldoc` utility included with `perl` will process this documentation into text, HTML, LaTeX, and so on.

Next there's an `index` subroutine. Following that is some more documentation and a `__PACKAGE__->meta->make_immutable`. It tells Moose that this module will not change at runtime. This statement is necessary for performance gains and is good practice to mention in every Moose module. Moose is covered in Chapter 8 in more detail. This statement is followed by `1`. The `1` is important to Perl for historical reasons and must not be removed. Modules must return `true` when they're loaded, otherwise Perl will assume that the loading has failed and will die with an error message. `1` is always `true`, so it's conventional to use it for this purpose.

Let us check what just happened by running the server with the following command:

```
perl script/myapp_server.pl
```

You will see something like the following besides the debug information you saw earlier:

```
[debug] Loaded Path actions:
.---------------------------------------+-------------------------------
----.
| Path                                  | Private
|
+---------------------------------------+-------------------------------
----+
| /                                     | /index
|
| /                                     | /default
|
| /hello                                | /hello/index
|
```

Opening the URL `http://localhost:3000/hello` will show you the following:

```
Matched MyApp::Controller::Hello in Hello
```

Adding a View

Now that the URL is mapped to the Controller method as expected, let us try something more challenging and show some HTML content. Instead of writing the HTML inside the response body as in the previous example, in this section, we will use a View. A View is a system that defines how content will be rendered. For this book, we will mostly be using the TT view which is based on a templating package, TT, that is available for any Perl program independent of Catalyst. To learn more about the TT package, visit `http://template-toolkit.org/`.

In the Controller method (sub index in `Hello.pm`), we will remove the line `$c->response->body()`. So, the Controller method looks like the following:

```
sub index :Path :Args(0) {
    my ( $self, $c ) = @_;

}
```

Please note that Catalyst takes care of forwarding the response to the default view after the Controller's execution. Later in this chapter, we will discover how Catalyst handles that and how it can be manipulated.

Let us create a View (using TT as mentioned) that the application can use as the default view.

The Template Toolkit module is included with the `Catalyst::Devel` package, so you should already have it. You'll need to install the Catalyst interface to it though by running the following command line:

```
$ cpan -i Catalyst::View::TT
```

If you don't have TT for some reason, cpan will detect that and install it for you. Once that's complete, create the View by running the following command line:

```
$ perl script/myapp_create.pl view TT TT
```

You will see something like this following:

```
$ perl script/myapp_create.pl view TT TT
 exists "/Volumes/Home/Users/solar/Projects/CatalystBook/MyApp/script/../
lib/MyApp/View"
 exists "/Volumes/Home/Users/solar/Projects/CatalystBook/MyApp/script/../
t"
created "/Volumes/Home/Users/solar/Projects/CatalystBook/MyApp/script/../
lib/MyApp/View/TT.pm"
created "/Volumes/Home/Users/solar/Projects/CatalystBook/MyApp/script/../
t/view_TT.t"
```

The TT TT part of the previous command means to create a View called View/TT.pm (the first TT) based on the standard Catalyst::View::TT (the second TT). This technically means you can have multiple views of Catalyst::View::TT with different names. You can choose any valid Perl filename as the name of your View (the first TT), but a simple TT makes the most sense here. For more complex applications with multiple views, it is a best practice to name them after the purpose they fulfill such as HTML or JSON.

Next, it's a good idea to add Catalyst::View::TT to the prerequisites section of Makefile.PL. Your application will run fine if you omit this step, but if you're diligent about adding your prerequisites to Makefile.PL, it will be very easy to move your application to another machine. A simple perl Makefile.PL && make on the new machine will allow Catalyst to automatically install all of your application's dependencies while you have a cup of coffee and relax. A minute of your time here will save much more time later.

Currently, the `Makefile.PL` looks something like the following:

```
#!/usr/bin/env perl
# IMPORTANT: if you delete this file your app will not work as
# expected.  You have been warned.
use inc::Module::Install;
use Module::Install::Catalyst; # Complain loudly if you don't have
                               # Catalyst::Devel installed or haven't
said
                               # 'make dist' to create a standalone
tarball.
name 'MyApp';
all_from 'lib/MyApp.pm';
requires 'Catalyst::Runtime' => '5.80021';
requires 'Catalyst::Plugin::ConfigLoader';
requires 'Catalyst::Plugin::Static::Simple';
requires 'Catalyst::Action::RenderView';
requires 'Moose';
requires 'namespace::autoclean';
requires 'Config::General'; # This should reflect the config file
format you've chosen
                   # See Catalyst::Plugin::ConfigLoader for supported
formats
test_requires 'Test::More' => '0.88';
catalyst;
install_script glob('script/*.pl');
auto_install;
WriteAll;
```

All you need to do to add a prerequisite is add a line of code like:

```
requires 'Catalyst::View::TT' => 0;
```

near the other `requires` statements in the previous code snippet (order isn't important). The `0` represents the minimum version of the module that your application requires. Leaving it at `0` is fine if you don't know the version, but it's best to specify the current version you're using to develop with. You can determine the version of any module on your system by typing the following line of code:

```
perl -MSome::Module -e 'print Some::Module->VERSION'
```

The next step is to create a template in the `root/hello` directory. For this example, we're going to create a page that says "Hello, world!", so let's call it `root/hello/index.tt`. The `root` directory is the default place where `Catalyst::View::TT` will look for templates. This can be changed by configuration if you really need to.

Here's the code to use in `index.tt`:

```
<?xml version="1.0" encoding="utf-8"?>
<!DOCTYPE html PUBLIC "-//W3C//DTD XHTML 1.1//EN" "http://www.w3.org/
TR/xhtml11/DTD/xhtml11.dtd">
<html xmlns="http://www.w3.org/1999/xhtml" xml:lang="en">
<head>
<title>Hello, world!</title>
</head>
<body>
<h1>Hello, world.</h1>
<p>
Here's a word from our Controller: [% word | html %].
</p>
</body>
</html>
```

This is just a regular XHTML file, with some special control sequences for Template Toolkit.

`[% word%]` tells TT to get the value of a variable called "word" and display it at that point in the template. The `| html` part after `word` in the example is a TT filter that means to escape any HTML in `word` so that < is rendered as an actual < sign and not an HTML tag. This prevents a type of security hole called **cross-site scripting** (**XSS**). While security probably isn't important for a "hello world" page, it's wise to get into good habits now.

Run the server, as explained, by typing `perl script/myapp_server.pl`, and open the page `http://localhost/hello`.

Right now, this `index.tt` will show the following:

Hello, world.

Here's a word from our Controller:

Note that nothing is rendered in the place of `[% word | html %]`. This is because we haven't set that variable "word" in the Controller. Such variables that are passed between Controllers and Views are called **stash**.

We can set the stash in the Controller by modifying the code to the following:

```
sub index :Path :Args(0) {
    my ( $self, $c) = @;
    $c->stash->{word} = "Bonjour!";
}
```

Now open `http://localhost:3000/hello`, and you will see the following:

Hello, world.

Here's a word from our Controller: Bonjour!.

Note that the word set in the stash for the variable `word` is now rendered instead of `[% word | html %]`.

More on Controller methods

In this section, we will discover the available flexibility on method declaration and URL mapping. We will start by trying to change the last example to accept an argument from the URL that it can render instead of **Bonjour!**

We can start by modifying the index subroutine. If we have to pass an argument `Hello/index/dsads`, then we can change the code to the following:

```
sub index :Path :Args(1) {
  my ( $self, $c, @args ) = @_; //Store the argument(s) from the URL
    in the list @args
  $c->stash->{word} = $args[0];
}
```

Notice that we have changed `Args(0)` to `Args(1)`. This will accept the argument after `index`. The URL `/hello` is derived from the name of the Controller with colons converted to `/` and the `Hello` from `Hello.pm` converted to all lowercase. The `:Path` attribute after `index` tells Catalyst that this method will handle URL requests that do not mention the method name such as `/hello`. The `Args(1)` attribute declares that this action expects one argument.

Now if you run the server and open a URL like `http://localhost:3000/hello/Bonjour!`, then you will see the following output:

Hello, world.

Here's a word from our Controller: Bonjour!.

Notice that the `[% word | html %]` is replaced with `Bonjour!`. Change `Bonjour!` to another word in the URL and that word should show up.

Congratulations! You have created your first dynamic Catalyst application.

If we specified :Local instead of :Path, then Catalyst would map the index action to handle a URL that looks like /hello/index. So, the URL looks like the following http://localhost/hello/index/Bonjour!, where Bonjour! is the argument that is being passed to the Controller. If we omitted the attributes (:Local, :Path, and so on), Catalyst would ignore the action entirely and it would be a normal Perl subroutine in the package. If we want to handle any URL with this method, then we can use the :Global attribute.

We also changed the first line of the hello subroutine to receive the parameter within the method. Initially, it looked like my ($self, $c) = @_;. This gets the first two arguments passed to the action by Catalyst, $self and $c.

$self is a MyApp::Controller::Hello object and is not of much use right now. $c is the Catalyst context and contains all the information about our application and the current request (and therefore is very useful). Catalyst passes more than just $self and $c though, so we want to modify that line to read my ($self, $c, @args)=@_;. This will allow us to access the rest of the arguments via the @args array.

Arguments are everything in the URL that Catalyst didn't use when matching an action. As an example, /hello/foo would invoke the action matching /hello followed by one argument (if we defined index as :Global above, it would accept any number of arguments. That is /hello/foo/bar will match the index method and consider foo and bar as two arguments). These two arguments will be passed to the action and will be available in the @args variable that you specified.

When you run the Catalyst server, you would see something like the following in the log:

```
[debug] Loaded Path actions:
.----------------------------------------+----------------------------------.
| Path                                   | Private                          |
|                                        |                                  |
+----------------------------------------+----------------------------------+
| /                                      | /index                           |
|                                        |                                  |
| /                                      | /default                         |
|                                        |                                  |
| /hello                                 | /hello/index                     |
|                                        |                                  |
'----------------------------------------+----------------------------------'
```

Notice that this table has two columns, Path and Private. Path is what you can mention in the URL and Private is which Controller (hello.pm) and method (sub index) it would get mapped to.

Let us revise what just happened:

```
my ( $self, $c, @args ) = @_;
my $word = $args[0] || 'Default word';
$c->stash->{word}  = $word;
```

The first line receives all the arguments from the URL in @args.

The second line assigns the first argument to a variable called word (or uses Default Word if there isn't a first argument). Finally, we put $word in the stash as word, so the [% word %] statement in our template can access that variable.

The template that will be rendered is determined by the private name of your action. In this case, the action /hello/hello will be attempted to be rendered with root/ hello/hello.tt. If you haven't set $c->response->body yet, the default View will be called to render the template. If you have more than one View, you will have to configure a default one by setting the default_view option in your config file to the name of your View. In this example, it would be "TT".

The View will then proceed to look for a stash variable named template that you can set to force a particular template to be rendered. If none is found, then it will use the private path of your action (not the public URI that dispatches to your action, but the /hello/everything path consisting of the Controller and action name) and append .tt as extension. It will look for this hello/hello.tt in the default template include path, which is root.

The *stash* is a data structure that exists throughout a single Catalyst request. Data you insert into the stash in an action will be available to the View (and other actions). Templates can only access variables that have been explicitly placed here, so it's important to remember to put your useful data in the stash (otherwise it will be gone at the end of the subroutine in the Controller, instead of at the end of the request).

If you're interested in experimenting some more with this setup, here are some things to try. Edit the hello.tt template to change the look of the page. You shouldn't even need to restart your development server for changes to take effect. After that, add another page to your application by creating another subroutine in Hello.pm and another template. Editing Hello.pm will require a restart, but you can automatically restart the server when necessary by running the server like perl script/myapp_server.pl -r -d. The -r will cause the server to restart when appropriate, and the -d will show debugging information, even if you've turned it off inside your application. This is especially useful as you will want to deactivate the hardcoded -Debug option in your MyApp.pm, once you are ready to deploy your application.

Some technical details

At this point, you may be wondering why the `hello.tt` template showed up without your code ever calling any methods in the Template Toolkit View. This is because the `end` action in the default `Root.pm` uses an ActionClass called RenderView. The `end` action in Root is called at the end of every request, and the `RenderView ActionClass` will automatically forward to the default View. If you'd rather be explicit about invoking the View, then you can add a line like:

```
$c->forward('View::TT');
```

at the end of your action (`RenderView` will stay out of the way). You can also set a `default_view` config option for a general default View, or set a stash variable named `current_view` to the name of the View you want to forward to for the current request only. If you have more than one View you should always explicitly forward or set any of these variables, as currently there's no rigorous definition of "default". You can make every action in a single Controller forward to the same View by overriding the `end` action in that Controller as follows:

```
sub end : Private {
  my ($self, $c) = @_;
  $c->forward('View::TT');
}
```

If you override `end` like this, the default `end` in `Root.pm` will not be called. (Only one `end` action is executed per request—the one that's "closest" to the action that started the request cycle.)

`end` actions (as well as the similar `begin` and `auto` actions) will be covered in more detail throughout the book.

Adding a database

The other component that many web applications require is a SQL relational database. Technically whatever ways are available to Perl for accessing databases, Catalyst has them all. The most popular is via an **Object-relational mapper (ORM)** called DBIx::Class (DBIC). Object-relational mappers allow you to perform operations on your database as though each database object were a Perl object. This means that instead of writing SQL like `SELECT * FROM table`, you can instead say `@results = $table_resultset->all`. The advantage of this approach is that DBIC handles the SQL for you, so you can switch from SQLite to DB2 without modifying any of your code. The resulting code in your Controller is also more readable; everything looks like a manipulation of Perl objects and data structures. We'll see the power of this approach throughout the book, but for now, let's just create a simple DBIC Model.

You can use any database that you like for this, but I recommend SQLite for development. SQLite is an "embedded" database, so the database exists as a single file and requires no server to run.

Installing SQLite

The first step is to install SQLite from the SQLite website at `http://sqlite.org/` (or through your distribution's package manager, the package is usually called "sqlite3"). You'll also need to install the Perl version of SQLite, called `DBD::SQLite`, and `DBIx::Class` itself as well as an adapter that will link our database schema definition to the Catalyst application. You can install these, except for SQLite, using `cpan` with the following:

```
$ cpan -i DBD::SQLite DBIx::Class Catalyst::Model::DBIC::Schema
```

Creating a database schema

Once the dependencies are installed, we'll create a sample database with the `sqlite3` command-line utility:

```
$ sqlite3 tmp/database
SQLite version 3.3.8
Enter ".help" for instructions
sqlite> CREATE TABLE test (id INTEGER PRIMARY KEY, subject TEXT, message
TEXT, date DATETIME);
sqlite> INSERT INTO test (id, subject, message, date) VALUES(NULL, "test
message", "this is a test message", "2005-01-01 00:00");
sqlite> INSERT INTO test (id, subject, message, date) VALUES(NULL,
"another test message", "this is a another test message, hooray", "2005-
01-01 00:01");
sqlite> SELECT * FROM test;
1|test message|this is a test message|2005-01-01 00:00
2|another test message|this is a another test message, hooray|2005-01-01
00:01
sqlite> .quit
$
```

Here we created a `test` table in a database file called `tmp/database` and added two rows to it.

SQLite has unusual semantics for auto-incrementing primary keys. You must declare the auto-increment column exactly as "INTEGER PRIMARY KEY" and then assign NULL during INSERT operations. DBIC will handle this automatically, but you should be aware of this unconventional approach when interacting with the database from within the `sqlite3` utility.

Creating a database model for Catalyst

To use this database from Catalyst, we need to create a Catalyst Model. We can do this using the following command line:

```
$ perl script/myapp_create.pl model TestDatabase DBIC::Schema MyApp::
Schema::TestDatabase create=dynamic dbi:SQLite:tmp/database
```

If you are on Windows, you may want to be careful in replacing / with \ whenever filesystems are referred.

The first argument is the name of the Catalyst Model (`TestDatabase`). `DBIC::Schema` is what sort of model we're creating. `MyApp::Schema::TestDatabase` is where the schema definition will be stored (we won't use the Schema in this example, but real applications will). `create=dynamic` tells DBIC to read the database every time the application is started to determine the schema (layout of tables, foreign key relations, and so on.). The final argument is the *DBI* connect string for the database.

Using the Model

We'll also create another Controller to learn to create a database Model as follows:

```
$ perl script/myapp_create.pl controller Database
```

Now, we'll want to create code to show this template in the `Database.pm` Controller. In this case, using the `index` action that's automatically generated will be fine.

We will need to populate a variable called `messages` with the data from our database. The code to do this looks like the following:

```
sub index :Path Args(0) {
  # same as index :Private my ( $self, $c ) = @_;
  $c->stash->{messages} = $c->model('TestDatabase::test')->search({});
}
```

This is almost the same as our hello action, but in this case we fill the `messages` variable with the entries in the `test` table (in the `TestDatabase` Model). The `$c->model(...)` syntax allows you to access any Model by name. `DBIC::Schema` supports extra syntax to allow you to name a table in the database directly (the `::test` part), so we use that to create a **ResultSet** object. The `ResultSet` is an iterator object that will only access the database when it is required; this is to make sure it doesn't fetch any data that isn't required by the application. The `->search({})` part will make sure that you receive a fresh `ResultSet` object.

Once we have this, we'll create a template to show data from the database in a file called `root/database/index.tt`. It should look like the following:

```
<?xml version="1.0" encoding="utf-8"?>
<!DOCTYPE html PUBLIC "-//W3C//DTD XHTML 1.1//EN" "http://www.w3.org/
TR/xhtml11/DTD/xhtml11.dtd">
<htmlxmlns="http://www.w3.org/1999/xhtml" xml:lang="en">
<head>
<title>Hello, database!</title>
</head>
<body>
<h1>Database</h1>
<p>Here's what the database looks like: </p>
<ol>
[% WHILE (message = messages.next) %]
<li>
<p>Message <b>[% message.subject | html %]</b> (#[% message.id | html
%]):</p>
<p>[% message.message | html %]</p>
<p>Written at <i>[% message.date | html %]</i>.</p>
</li>
[% END %]
</ol>
</body>
</html>
```

The `[% WHILE (message = messages.next) %]` command loops over each row in the `ResultSet` for the `test` table, and creates a variable called `message` that holds that row. The other `[% ... %]` commands in the template simply extract the data from the row via the column name. That's all there is to it—Catalyst handles the hard stuff for you!

To view your database as an HTML page, start the development server again and browse to `http://localhost:3000/database`.

You will see something like the following:

Summary

In this chapter, we created our first Catalyst application with the `catalyst.pl` utility. After running the skeleton application and inspecting it with a web browser, we added an HTML template View with the `myapp_create.pl` script and created a "Hello" Controller to display a "Hello, world" page. Finally, we added a database Model using `DBIC::Schema` and created a Controller containing actions that show data from the database, via the View and templates, as an HTML page.

3
Building a Real Application

In this chapter, we're going to build our first real application—an address book. We'll start with a skeleton similar to the application from the last chapter, but then we'll add some real logic to create a **CRUD** (create, retrieve, update, delete) interface to a database. We'll learn how to define forms that automatically generate and validate themselves and how to design a database schema. We'll also use a View that generates common pages for us, so we won't have to worry about stylesheets or tricky HTML for now.

Environment setup

Before we start writing our new application, we'll need to create a skeleton again. We can create it using the following commands:

```
$ catalyst.pl AddressBook
```

```
$ cd AddressBook/
```

We'll also need two more CPAN modules for this chapter. These can be installed from CPAN using the following command:

```
$ cpan Catalyst::Controller::FormBuilder Catalyst::Controller::BindLex
```

> This should really use `FormHandler`, which is a Moose-based form handling framework that allows one to use nice object-oriented classes. `FormHandler` is actively maintained while `FormBuilder` hasn't been updated since 2007. `BindLex` has also been deprecated for a while, I think even by its author.

The previous command will ensure that the latest version of each module is installed on your system. After installing the modules, we'll add a special Template Toolkit View called `TTSite` to our application, using the following command:

```
$ perl script/addressbook_create.pl view HTML TTSite
```

`TTSite` will automatically generate some basic HTML for us, so our templates will only need to contain the text and markup that applies specifically to them. The header, footer, messages, and stylesheets will all be handled automatically and will be easy to customize later.

Database design

The first real step will be to think about what kind of data we need to store and then design a database schema to efficiently store that data. To keep things simple (but realistic), let's set our specification as follows:

- The address book should keep track of multiple addresses for a person
- Each person can have a first and last name
- Each address can have a street address, a phone number, and an e-mail address

Translated into a relational database schema, that means we'll have a `people` table that will assign a unique identifier to each `firstname` and `lastname` pair.

Then we'll have an `addresses` table that will allow each person to have multiple addresses, each consisting of a unique ID (so it's easy to reference later), a `location` ("Office", "Home"), a free-form postal address (so we don't have to worry about the complexity of having a city, country, state, postal code, and so on), a phone number, and an e-mail address. Each row will have a column called `person`, which will be the ID of the person that "owns" this address (called a **foreign key** in SQL parlance). We'll also make each field in the `addresses` table optional (except for the `location`), so that we can have locations like "Mobile" for storing a mobile phone number (without a postal address or e-mail).

Now we just have to express this as SQL, and type it into SQLite as follows:

```
$ sqlite3 tmp/database
sqlite> CREATE TABLE people (id INTEGER NOT NULL PRIMARY KEY, firstname
VARCHAR(50) NOT NULL, lastname VARCHAR(50) NOT NULL);
sqlite> CREATE TABLE addresses (id INTEGER NOT NULL PRIMARY KEY, person
INTEGER NOT NULL, location VARCHAR(20), postal TEXT, phone VARCHAR(20),
email VARCHAR(100));
```

Let's also add some sample data, so that we can create a "view" page and actually see some data show up as follows:

```
sqlite> INSERT INTO people VALUES(NULL, 'Your', 'Name');
sqlite> INSERT INTO addresses VALUES(NULL, 1, 'Home', '123 Green St.',
'123-456-7890', 'home@example.com');
sqlite> INSERT INTO addresses VALUES(NULL, 1, 'Work', '42 Work St.',
'987-654-3210', 'work@example.com');
sqlite> .quit
```

With the schema configured, let's link the database to a Catalyst Model using the following command:

```
$ perl script/addressbook_create.pl model AddressDB DBIC::Schema
AddressBook::Schema::AddressDB create=static dbi:SQLite:database
```

This will create a Model called AddressDB, and it will also create a Schema/ AddressDB subdirectory that contains the definition of our database schema in DBIx::Class's (DBIC) format. This schema will be pre-populated with the schema we just created with the sqlite3 utility. Keeping the schema in this format will allow us to deploy to any database system that DBIx::Class supports by simply running the deploy function in your schema. It will also let us explicitly specify any relations between the tables, so that we can access the data from inside our program in a natural way. This will also allow functionality, like automatically deleting a person's addresses when we delete that person. At this stage, you can do a quick sanity check and see if the contents of the file lib/AddressBook/Schema/ AddressDB.pm have the following:

```
__PACKAGE__->config(
    schema_class => 'AddressBook::Schema::AddressDB',
    connect_info => [
        'dbi:SQLite:database',

    ],
);
```

Understanding the interface to the database

The exact files generated (inside `lib/AddressBook`) are:

- `Model/AddressDB.pm`: The actual Model that Catalyst uses. It's simply a stub that points `DBIx::Class` at the `Schema/AddressDB.pm` schema. This file also contains the database details like the type of database, driver used, database name, and any username and password, as required.

- `Schema/AddressDB.pm`: This is the schema that the Model points to. This is another stub that automatically loads everything in the subdirectory `/AddressDB`.

- `Schema/AddressDB/Result/People.pm` and `Schema/AddressDB/Result/Addresses.pm`: This is where the real schema data is stored. Each of these files will declare a table name (so that Perl knows that `People.pm` is the `people` table in the database) and the column definitions. Relationships between tables are added here, as are any specific access methods you'd like to add. Accessing a column's data by name is available by default, so most people won't need to add their own methods.

We'll need to dig inside these schema files so that we can specify the relations. Let's look at `People.pm` first.

```
package AddressBook::Schema::AddressDB::Result::People;
use strict;
use warnings;
use base 'DBIx::Class';
__PACKAGE__->load_components("InflateColumn::DateTime", "Core");
__PACKAGE__->table("people");
__PACKAGE__->add_columns(
  "id",
  {
    data_type => "INTEGER",
    default_value => undef,
    is_nullable => 0,
    size => undef,
  },
  "firstname",
  {
    data_type => "VARCHAR",
    default_value => undef,
    is_nullable => 0,
    size => 50,
```

```
    },
    "lastname",
    {
      data_type => "VARCHAR",
      default_value => undef,
      is_nullable => 0,
      size => 50,
    },
);
__PACKAGE__->set_primary_key("id");
# Created by DBIx::Class::Schema::Loader v0.04005 @ 2010-04-05
13:32:11
# DO NOT MODIFY THIS OR ANYTHING ABOVE! md5sum:QkLmUWW4Wzn1jeowkWCmNQ
# You can replace this text with custom content, and it will be
preserved on regeneration
1;
```

The generated structure is just like any other Perl module with the difference that `DBIx::Class` is used as a base class. The Dbic class `InflateColumn::DateTime` helps in the creation and updating of timestamps for every record whenever they are created and modified. `__PACKAGE__->table("people")` configures this schema module to represent the table `people` in the database. The statements following the package configurations define all the columns in the database. The following line of code is used to set a column as the primary key in the table:

```
__PACKAGE__->set_primary_key("id");
```

Once you have created a Perl module or Dbix schema that represents the tables in the database, use the Catalyst helper scripts as we did. You will most of the time, find it necessary to add more details to the schema. This may include relationship between tables and specific properties for each field. Or even custom functions that can be used to perform simple to complex operations on the Model.

Now you may wonder what would happen if a lot of changes are made manually and then you have a necessity to change the table structure in the database itself. Then you may want to run the helper script again to update the modules with the new table(s) structure. Therefore, there is a possibility of loosing any manual change done on the schema files. Fortunately, the helper scripts take care of this. If you notice you will find two lines similar to the following in every schema module that was generated:

```
# Created by DBIx::Class::Schema::Loader v0.04005 @ 2009-10-20
08:19:50
# DO NOT MODIFY THIS OR ANYTHING ABOVE! md5sum:BrDBAn7IgMoeBHW8UOCYLw
```

Whatever is placed after these lines is preserved even when the schema files are being updated by the helper scripts.

Now, let us look at our example. As every entry in this table can have zero or more addresses (entries in the `addresses` table) associated with it, it would be useful to access these addresses as though they were data stored in a column (like the `firstname`). In SQL, this is called a "has many" relationship and we use the `has_many` class method to make `DBIx::Class` aware of this relationship.

```
__PACKAGE__->has_many(
  addresses => 'AddressBook::Schema::AddressDB::Result::Addresses',
    'person',
{cascading_delete => 1}  );
```

This looks pretty complicated, but it's just a matter of reading everything right. The last example is read as, "This *package* (module, table) **has many** *addresses* in the `AddressBook::Schema::AddressDB::Addresses` table". The column that relates addresses to this package is `person` in the `addresses` table.

To understand more about the different relationship configurations, you can refer to the following URL:

```
http://search.cpan.org/~frew/DBIx-Class-0.08121/lib/DBIx/Class/
Relationship.pm
```

`{cascading_delete => 1}` is a configuration option that causes any address associated with a person to be deleted when that person is deleted. The name `addresses` we chose is the name we'll use to access the related data of a `person` object. It can be anything you want. It need not bear any resemblance to a column name in either of the affected tables.

We'll also add one method to this class as follows:

```
sub name {
  my $self = shift;
  return $self->firstname. ' '. $self->lastname;
}
```

This will allow us to access the full name of the person by simply calling `name` on an instance (much easier than concatenating the `firstname` and `lastname` every time we want to display them together).

Once that's set, we need to do the same things for the auto-generated `Addresses.pm`. The code for this file looks pretty much the same as the `People.pm` file. It is given as follows:

```perl
package AddressBook::Schema::AddressDB::Result::Addresses;
use strict;
use warnings;
use base 'DBIx::Class';
__PACKAGE__->load_components("InflateColumn::DateTime", "Core");
__PACKAGE__->table("addresses");
__PACKAGE__->add_columns(
  "id",
  {
    data_type => "INTEGER",
    default_value => undef,
    is_nullable => 0,
    size => undef,
  },
  "person",
  {
    data_type => "INTEGER",
    default_value => undef,
    is_nullable => 0,
    size => undef,
  },
  "location",
  {
    data_type => "VARCHAR",
    default_value => undef,
    is_nullable => 1,
    size => 20,
  },
  "postal",
  {
    data_type => "TEXT",
    default_value => undef,
    is_nullable => 1,
    size => undef,
  },
  "phone",
  {
    data_type => "VARCHAR",
    default_value => undef,
    is_nullable => 1,
```

```
    size => 20,
  },
  "email",
  {
    data_type => "VARCHAR",
    default_value => undef,
    is_nullable => 1,
    size => 100,
  },
);
__PACKAGE__->set_primary_key("id");
# Created by DBIx::Class::Schema::Loader v0.04005 @ 2010-04-05
13:32:11
# DO NOT MODIFY THIS OR ANYTHING ABOVE! md5sum:N/kFLKKfXHgpLqDgCGl9WA
# You can replace this text with custom content, and it will be
preserved on regeneration
1;
```

The only modification we need to make is to define a relation from `addresses` to `people`. This relation is called belongs_to relation and looks like the following:

```
__PACKAGE__->belongs_to(
person => 'AddressBook::Schema::AddressDB::Result::People');
```

This simply says that the `person` column in this table is a foreign key into the `AddressBook::Schema::AddressDB::Result::People` table. In terms of coding, this means that when we access `$some_address->person`, we will get the `person` object that this address is associated with instead of the database's ID number for that person.

That's all we need to do with the Model for this section. Let us put this aside for a moment and turn our focus to the View.

TTSite

`TTSite` is a Catalyst View that wraps every TT template we use in a header and footer. All of this happens transparently, so we can add some prettiness to our site without writing any CSS or HTML.

TTSite isn't really officially endorsed. It might be okay to use it, but it should be noted that building your own TT base view isn't that hard.

There are a few differences from the standard TT view to be aware of. First, templates are stored in /root/src instead of /root. TTSite keeps its configuration in /root/lib, so that's where you'll want to go if you want to change the look of the site. The configuration is easy to understand—the file called header contains the TT commands that will be added to the header of the page (and so on).

For this application, we need to make a few modifications to the default setup. First, let's remove the default "message" (to display at the top of the page), so we can specify our own from a Controller. To do this, edit /root/lib/config/main, removing the block of code that looks like this:

```
# set defaults for variables, etc. DEFAULT
message = 'There is no message';
```

Next, we'll edit the template that formats our main content so that it will show us a message if it exists (and an error message if one exists). In /root/lib/site/layout, add the following lines after the <div id="content"> and before the [% content %] command so that it looks like:

```
<div id="content">
[% IF error %]
<p><span class="error">[% error | html %]</span></p> [% END %]
[% IF message %]
<p><span class="message">[% message | html %]</span></p> [% END %]
[% content %]
```

This change will allow our Controllers to set messages (or errors) that will display above the content. This means we can skip the step of adding error screens or success screens. For example, after adding an address, we can return the user to the list of addresses and add a message saying *Address added successfully!*. This is in contrast to the traditional scheme of having an entire page with the message and a link to *go back*.

Finally, we need to edit /lib/AddressBook/View/HTML.pm and add a line to set the default template extension to .tt2. Simply add the following as a key/value to __PACKAGE__ config:

```
TEMPLATE_EXTENSION  => '.tt2',
```

so that it looks like the following:

```
__PACKAGE__->config({
    INCLUDE_PATH => [
        AddressBook->path_to( 'root', 'src' ),
        AddressBook->path_to( 'root', 'lib' )
    ],
```

```
        TEMPLATE_EXTENSION => '.tt2',
        PRE_PROCESS       => 'config/main',
        WRAPPER           => 'site/wrapper',
        ERROR             => 'error.tt2',
        TIMER             => 0
    });
```

This will cause Catalyst to automatically pick which template to render, based on the name of the action. For example, the action `/person/edit` will automatically use the template in `root/src/person/edit.tt2`, which will save us some typing later on.

That's all we need to get a comfortable View setup, so let's start adding some pages! If there is something that you have not understood in this section, it is a good idea to just proceed further and come back to this later. Most of what we did in this section are tweaks and changes which make things easier for us as we proceed.

Creating the index page

The first pages we need to add are an index page and a "Not Found" page. The index page goes in `/root/src/index.tt2` and looks like the following:

```
    [% META title = "Welcome to the Address Book" %]
    <p>Here you will find All Things Address.</p>
    <p>From here, you can:
      <ul>
        <li>
          <a href="[% c.uri_for_action('/person/list') %]">Look at all
            people</a>
        </li>
        <li>
          <a href="[% c.uri_for_action('/person/add') %]">Add a new
            person</a>
        </li>
      </ul>
    </p>
```

(This is the template that will get rendered by default when the index method in the root Controller is executed.)

As you can see, TTSite saved us a bit of work here. All we have to do is set the title, and then provide the content. In this case, we're just printing out two links, one to list all people and another to add a new person. Note that instead of specifying URLs directly, we use c.uri_for_action and then the internal name of the action (displayed in the debugging output). This ensures that the URL that's generated will always be correct, even if your application is moved to a different host or subdirectory, or if you change your action from Local to Global, or something similar.

Creating a "Not Found" page

Next, we need a "Not Found" page to be shown to the user when they enter an invalid URL. We'll call this not_found.tt2, and it will live in the same directory as index.tt2:

```
[% META title = '404 Not Found' %]
<p>We couldn't find the page you were looking for. Maybe you'd like to
<a href="[% c.uri_for('/') %]">go home</a> instead?
</p>
```

Now that we have the templates, we need to add some actions in the Root Controller that will show them when appropriate. The code in /lib/AddressBook/ Controller/Root.pm should look like the following (replacing the auto-generated default and index actions, but nothing else):

```
sub default : Path {

    my ( $self, $c ) = @_;
    $c->response->status('404');
    $c->stash->{template} = 'not_found.tt2';
}
sub index : Path Args(0) {};
```

This is the same thing that we did in the last chapter, except in the index action we don't do anything, as TTSite will automatically render index.tt2 when the index action is called. In default, we are displaying the not found.tt2 template for every action that is not matched with any other action Controller.

With that, we're ready to take a first look at our application. Start up the development server using the following command:

```
$ perl script/addressbook_server.pl -r -d
```

Then navigate to `http://localhost:3000/`. The index page should show up like the following:

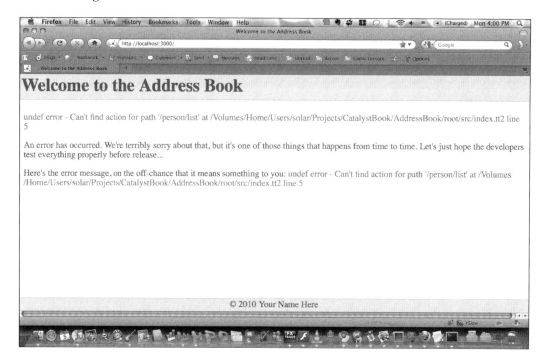

It is appropriate to get the error that you see in the screenshot, as you do not yet have the `people` Controller. The View is merely complaining that such an action `/person/list` doesn't exist. (Remember: `<li><a href="[% c.uri_for_action('/person/list') %]">Look at all people</a></li>`).

Then navigate to `http://localhost:3000/this/does/not/exist`. You should see the error page and be able to click a link to get back to the index page.

If that works, we're ready to start writing the real code!

Viewing people

The first link on the index page is **Look at all people**. So let's create an action that will display everyone in our database, along with their addresses (if any). We'll also show links to relevant actions such as "edit name", "add address", and "delete person". The eventual goal is to have a page that looks something like the following screenshot:

The page is a little busy, but it conveys all the information that we want to know. (You'll also notice that Catalyst and Perl can handle Unicode data flawlessly.)

The first thing we need to do is to create a `Person` Controller for managing people. This Controller will have add, delete, and list actions for each person. (The list action actually shows every person, which is convenient even if the grammar isn't perfect.)

Let us generate a Controller for `Person` using the helpers, as follows:

```
perl script/addressbook_create.pl controller Person
```

It should look like the following (minus comments):

```
package AddressBook::Controller::Person;
use Moose;
use namespace::autoclean;
BEGIN {extends 'Catalyst::Controller'; }
sub index :Path :Args(0) {
```

```
    my ( $self, $c ) = @_;
    $c->response->body('Matched AddressBook::Controller::Person in
Person.');
}
__PACKAGE__->meta->make_immutable;
1;
  Let's change the sub index controller method to the following
sub list : Local {
my ($self, $c) = @_;
my $people = $c->model('AddressDB::People');
$c->stash->{people} = $people;
}
1;
```

Here, the local `list` action gets all the `People` out of the database and stores them in `$people` (and then in `$c->stash->{people}`) and we're done.

That's all the Controller needs to do to create a page like the one in the last screenshot. Now, we just need the `list.tt2` template inside `root/src/person/list.tt2`:

```
[% META title = 'People' %]
[% IF people.count > 0 %]
<p>Here are people that I know about:</p>
<ul>
  [% WHILE (person = people.next) %]
  <li>
    [% person.name | html %]
    <a href="[% c.uri_for("/address/add/$person.id") | html %]">Add
      address</a>
    <a href="[% c.uri_for("/person/edit/$person.id") | html %]">Edit</
a>
    <a href="[% c.uri_for("/person/delete/$person.id") | html
%]">Delete</a>
    [% SET addresses = person.addresses %]
    <ul>
      [% FOREACH address = addresses %]
      <li>
        <b>[% address.location | html  %]</b>
        <a href="[% c.uri_for("/address/edit/$address.id") | html
          %]">Edit</a>
        <a href="[% c.uri_for("/address/delete/$address.id") | html
          %]">Delete</a>
        <br />
        <address>
          [% address.postal | html | html_line_break %]
```

```
          </address>
          Phone: [% address.phone | html %]<br /> Email: [% address.
email | html %]<br />
        </li>
        [% END %]
      </ul>
    </li>
    [% END %]
  </ul>
  [% ELSE %]
  <p>No people yet!</p> [% END %]
  <p><a href="[% c.uri_for("/person/add") | html %]"> Add a new
  person...
  </a></p>
  </li>
```

This looks fairly complex, but it's mostly HTML that makes the data from the database look nice. The bulk of the code consists of a WHILE loop that iterates over each Person in the database. Once we have a Person object, we can print out the first name, last name, and some links to pages where we can edit and delete people and addresses (we'll create these pages later). After that, we get an array of addresses associated with this person (from the relationship we added to the schema earlier in the chapter). We iterate over each element in that array and print out the location, postal address, phone number, and e-mail address associated to that address. When there are no more addresses, we return to the WHILE loop and get the next person in the database. This continues until everything in the database has been printed.

To see this in action, start up the server, add some new people and addresses to the database (via the sqlite3 utility), and watch them appear on the page at http://localhost:3000/person/list.

Basic CRUD

Let's start by writing the easiest method, a method to delete a person from the database. All we need is a simple action in the Person Controller. (Note: The order of the methods in the Person.pm file does not matter. You can add this method before or after sub index{ }):

```
sub delete : Local {
  my ($self, $c, $id) = @_;
  my $person = $c->model('AddressDB::People')->
  find({id => $id});
  $c->stash->{person} = $person;
```

```
    if($person){
      $c->stash->{message} = 'Deleted '. $person->name;
      $person->delete;
    }
    else {
      $c->response->status(404);
      $c->stash->{error} = "No person $id";
    }
    $c->forward('list');
}
```

This action will create a URL that looks like /person/delete/1, where 1 is the person's ID number in the database. Using that ID number that's passed in the URL, we look for the row in the database with that ID. If we find one, we set the status message to Deleted Person's Name and then delete the person (the delete method will also remove any addresses that were associated with that person). If there's no person in the database matching that ID, we set an error message instead. As a good practice, we also set the status of the response in such a case as 404.

Regardless of the outcome, we go back to the list page we came from. There, the new data will show up, with an appropriate message at the top of the screen. This makes it very easy for the user to be sure that his/her action took effect—there's a message saying that it did and the user can look at the list of people and confirm that the person deleted is gone—and it makes it easy to perform another operation, as he/she doesn't have to navigate anywhere. The only disadvantage is that the URL in the URL bar is no longer correct. For now, we'll live with this, but in the next chapter, we'll see how to keep the URL correct and forward the user around in the same way.

Forms

Now that you've deleted the sample row that you added when you created the database, we'll need to implement methods for adding (and editing) a person. As creating and validating HTML forms is a repetitive and boring task (you can write your forms in HTML just like before if you like to), we're going to use Catalyst::Controller::FormBuilder to automatically build our forms. All we have to do is create a definition of the form, and FormBuilder will generate the HTML and validate it when the user submits it. If there's a problem with one of the fields, FormBuilder will return the form to the user with an appropriate message. If the user's browser supports JavaScript, FormBuilder will validate the form on the client side to save a round-trip. (The data will be validated again on the server and rejected if it's bad. This prevents users from turning off JavaScript and submitting bad data.)

Chapter 3

 There are other form builders like HTML::Builder that are gaining popularity. However, it is still widely used, simpler to learn, and well documented. I recommend you continue to use FormBuilder only till you master Catalyst enough to learn the emerging form builders.

Let's start by adding the "edit name" form. As the action will be located at /person/edit, the form definition will live in the /root/forms/person/edit.fb file. This file contains the following (indentation is important):

```
name: person_edit
method: post
fields:
  firstname:
    label: First Name
    type: text
    size: 30
    required: 1
  lastname:
    label: Last Name
    type: text
    size: 30

    required: 1
```

We'll also need a template where we can render this form, so inside /root/src/person/edit.tt2, we'll add a very small template:

```
[% META title = "Edit a person" %]
[%FormBuilder.render%]
```

This is all we need to generate a form for adding a person or changing a person's name. Before we add all the form logic, let's write a simple action in the Person Controller so that we can see what the form looks like:

```
sub edit : Local Form {
  my ($self, $c) = @_;
  my $form = $self->formbuilder;
  if ($form->submitted && $form->validate) {
    $c->stash->{message} = 'Thanks for submitting the form!';
  }
}
```

[57]

We also need to inherit from `Catalyst::Controller::FormBuilder` at the top of the Controller file using `extends 'Catalyst::Controller::FormBuilder'` like the following:

```
package AddressBook::Controller::Person;
use Moose;
use namespace::autoclean;
BEGIN {extends 'Catalyst::Controller'; }
extends 'Catalyst::Controller::FormBuilder';
```

Also, when using `FormBuilder`, please ensure to comment out the following line:

```
#__PACKAGE__->meta->make_immutable;
```

in the Controller to avoid Moose-related errors during initialization. Moose is explained in detail in Chapter 9.

You can now start up the development server and navigate to `http://localhost:3000/person/edit`. You should see the form that you defined in the `edit.fb` form definition file. Try entering some text and click submit. If your entries are acceptable (according to the constraints specified in the form definition), then `$form->validate` will return `true` and the message **Thanks for submitting the form!** will appear at the top of your page. If you manage to submit some invalid data (one of the names left blank, for example), then `FormBuilder` will bring you back to the form and mark the fields that have errors in red. Now that our form works, we just need to add some database logic to have a fully working action. The final action code looks like the following:

```
sub edit : Local Form {
  my ($self, $c, $id) = @_;
  my $form = $self->formbuilder;
  my $person = $c->model('AddressDB::People')->
  find_or_new({id => $id});
  if ($form->submitted && $form->validate) {
    # form was submitted and it validated
    $person->firstname($form->field('firstname'));
    $person->lastname ($form->field( 'lastname'));
    $person->update_or_insert;
    $c->stash->{message} =
    ($id > 0 ? 'Updated ' : 'Added ') . $person->name;
    $c->forward('list');
  }
  else {
    # first time through, or invalid form
    if(!$id){
```

```
        $c->stash->{message} = 'Adding a new person';
    }
    $form->field(name  => 'firstname',
    value => $person->firstname);
    $form->field(name  => 'lastname',
    value => $person->lastname);
  }
}
```

Here's what happens: The action is used to both display the form and handle the submitted values. It accepts the numeric ID of the person to edit. We use this ID number to view the person with that ID in the database via the `find_or_new` DBIC method. The `find` method by itself will work for locating existing records, but using `find_or_new` instead will create a new record if there's no matching record already in the database. The new record that is created is not actually written to the database; it only exists in memory. Only when we insert the record explicitly will it be created in the database. This allows us to call `find_or_new` each time the action is called because we only `insert_or_update` the record when we've verified that the data is valid. (If we used `find_or_create` instead of `find_or_new`, we'd create a record every time someone requested the form, as `find_or_create` will create an entry in the database immediately if the record does not exist. That would lead to a lot of useless data in the database. Whereas `find_or_new` will only create an entry in the database when explicitly asked to insert.)

After we have a record to manipulate, we check whether the form has been submitted (`$form->submitted`), and if so, whether the form data is valid according to the `edit.fb` file (`$form->validate`). If both of these conditions are `true`, we transfer the data from the form to the database and then `update_or_insert` the record (insert if the record is new, update if it already exists; DBIC will figure out which one is appropriate). Then, we add a message to the stash, and forward it to the list page (so the user can edit another person and see the new person along with the existing people).

If the form hasn't been submitted yet, or the data is not valid, we transfer the `firstname` and `lastname` from the database to the form and let `FormBuilder` display the form (again). Although we transfer the database information to the form each time, the submitted form data will override the database data. This can be prevented by passing the `force => 1` option to `$form->field`, in which case the database data will override the form data.

Although the `edit` action actually handles adding new entries, it's a good idea to have a separate `add` action as well. This will allow you to be flexible in the future; if you decide that the add form should be different from the edit form, you can make that change without finding all links to `edit` that actually add. (Make sure that you use `$c->uri_for('/person/add')` instead of `$c->uri_for('/person/edit')` when generating links. Even though they do the same thing now, they won't if you change the `add` action later.)

Here's the `add` action that redirects the user to the `edit` action:

```
sub add : Local {
  my ($self, $c) = @_;
  $c->response->redirect($c->uri_for_action('edit'));
}
```

If you'd prefer not to do a client-side redirect, you can add the following code instead:

```
sub add : Local Form('/person/edit') {
  my ($self, $c) = @_;
  $c->go('edit', []);
}
```

This makes for a cleaner application, but also for extra typing to get the same functionality.

The `[]` in the `go` statement tells Catalyst to throw away any arguments that were passed to the action. This way, visiting the URL `/person/add/2` will add a new person, not edit person #2.

Finishing up

The final feature we need to add to our address book is an address editing Controller, with methods for adding, editing, and deleting addresses. Even though the address data is more complicated than the simple `firstname`/`lastname` records that we were working with before, the code is almost exactly the same.

Let's start by creating a template for the address editing form in `root/src/address/edit.tt2`:

```
[% META title = "Address" %]
<p>Here's some text explaining the form below. Only the "location"
field is required, etc., etc.</p>
[%FormBuilder.render%]
```

This looks just like the name editing form. In a real application, you will want to add some text explaining the form so that your users know what constraints are placed on the data. As this is just another template, you can add as much text before or after the form as you think appropriate. You can also use variables from the stash and so on.

Next, we want to add a definition of the form in `root/forms/address/edit.fb`. This can be done in the following manner:

```
name: address_edit
method: POST
title: Address
fields:
  location:
  label: Location
  type: select
  options: Home, Office, Mobile
  other: 1
  required: 1
postal:
  label: Mailing Address type: textarea
  rows: 4
  cols: 60
phone:
  label: Phone Number
  validate: PHONE
email:
  label: E-Mail Address
  validate: EMAIL
```

In this form, we're taking advantage of some of the more advanced features of `FormBuidler`. The first field, `location`, is declared to be a drop-down menu with `Home`, `Office`, and `Mobile` as options. We also tell `FormBuilder` to provide an `other` option. This will create a text field that can be filled out to declare a location other than one of the options we explicitly mentioned. `FormBuilder` will automatically generate the JavaScript required to hide and unhide this field as appropriate.

The `phone` and `email` fields are also special. As we want to make sure that the user submits realistic phone numbers and e-mail addresses, we tell `FormBuilder` to use its built-in `EMAIL` and `PHONE` validators (see the `FormBuilder` documentation for a full list of validation types). If the built-in validation functions don't meet your needs, you can also specify a regular expression in single quotes instead. `FormBuilder` will generate the JavaScript equivalent of this regex for client-side validation and then use the regex as you specified it for the server-side validation. This is extremely convenient for complicated forms.

With that out of the way, all we need to do is create the Address Controller and write relevant logic.

You can create the Address Controller through the following line of code:

perl script/addressbook_create.pl Address

and add the following highlighted code to the Address Controller (lib/ AddressBook/Controller/Address.pm). Be sure to include FormBuilder and comment __PACKAGE__-->immutable as follows:

```
package AddressBook::Controller::Address;
use Moose;
use namespace::autoclean;
BEGIN {extends 'Catalyst::Controller'; }
extends 'Catalyst::Controller::FormBuilder';
=head1 NAME
AddressBook::Controller::Address - Catalyst Controller
=head1 DESCRIPTION
Catalyst Controller.
=head1 METHODS
=cut
=head2 index
=cut
sub add : Local Form('/address/edit') {
  my ($self, $c, $person_id) = @_;
  $c->go('edit', [undef, $person_id]);}
sub edit : Local Form {
  my ($self, $c, $address_id, $person_id) = @_;
  my $form = $self->formbuilder;
  my $address;

  if (!$address_id && $person_id) {
    # we're adding a new address to $person
    # check that person exists
    my $person = $c->model('AddressDB::People')->find({id => $person_
id});
    if (!$person) {
      $c->stash->{error} = 'No such person!';
      $c->detach('/person/list');
    }
    # create the new address
    $address = $c->model('AddressDB::Addresses')->new({person =>
$person});
  }
```

```
    else {
      $address = $c->model('AddressDB::Addresses')->find({id =>
$address_id});
      if (!$address) {
        $c->stash->{error} = 'No such address!';
        $c->detach('/person/list');
      }
    }
  }
  if ($form->submitted && $form->validate) {
    # transfer data from form to database
    $address->location($form->field('location'));
    $address->postal  ($form->field('postal'        ));
    $address->phone  ($form->field('phone' ));
    $address->email  ($form->field('email' ));
    $address->insert_or_update;
    $c->stash->{message} =
      ($address_id > 0 ? 'Updated ' : 'Added new ').
      'address for '. $address->person->name;
    $c->detach('/person/list');
  }
  else {
    # transfer data from database to form
    $c->stash->{address} = $address;
    if (!$address_id) {
      $c->stash->{message} = 'Adding a new address ';
    }
    else {
      $c->stash->{message} = 'Updating an address ';
    }
    $c->stash->{message} .= ' for '. $address->person->name;
    $form->field(name  => 'location',
      value => $address->location);
    $form->field(name  => 'postal',
      value => $address->postal);
    $form->field(name  => 'phone',
      value => $address->phone);
    $form->field(name  => 'email',
      value => $address->email);
  }
}
sub delete : Local {
  my ($self, $c, $address_id) = @_;
```

```perl
    my $address = $c->model('AddressDB::Addresses')->
      find({id => $address_id});
    if ($address) {
      # "Deleted First Last's Home address"
      $c->stash->{message} =
        'Deleted ' . $address->person->name. q{'s }.
      $address->location. ' address';
      $address->delete;
    }
    else {
      $c->stash->{error} = 'No such address';
    }
    $c->forward('/person/list');
}
=head1 AUTHOR
Antano Solar John
=head1 LICENSE
This library is free software. You can redistribute it and/or modify
it under the same terms as Perl itself.
=cut
#__PACKAGE__->meta->make_immutable;
1;
```

This Controller employs the same techniques as the `Person.pm` Controller, but some of the details are different. First, the `edit` action accepts two arguments, the address' ID and the person's ID. This creates a URL like `/address/edit/0/5`, so that the edit action can also create new addresses. When we edit an address, we specify only the address ID. When we want to create an address, we leave the address ID undefined (or zero) and specify the person's ID instead. This is a little unwieldy, so we abstract these details out to the `add` action. The `add` action accepts the person's ID and then forwards the appropriate data to the `edit` action.

Once inside the `edit` action, we determine whether we're adding or editing. If we're adding, we create a new row in the database that's linked to the person that was passed in. Note that when we create the row, we assign the actual person object to the person column, not the person's ID number. Although the database actually stores the relation from an address to its person via an ID number, this is a detail that DBIC handles for us. We only have to think about what we mean, not how the database represents relations.

If it turns out that the person ID that was passed doesn't exist in the database, then we return the user to the list of people and addresses with an error message at the top. If we're instead editing an existing address, we just look up the address by the address ID number that was passed into the action. If we can't find one, we return the user to the list page with an error message.

At this point, we have an address object (existing or newly-created) that we can use to populate the form. The rest of the action looks just like the one for adding or editing a person, except that we have a few more fields this time.

The address deletion action also works exactly like the person deletion action, except we delete an `address` object instead of a `person` object.

As we already added code to list addresses to the `/person/list` template, we can restart the server, browse to that page (`http://localhost:3000/person/list`), and try adding some addresses. You should now have full creation, listing, editing, and deletion facilities, all tied together with a consistent look and feel.

Summary

In this chapter, we created a full CRUD application. We started by creating a database schema inside of SQLite. Then, we created a Catalyst model for accessing this database. As SQLite doesn't handle foreign key relations by itself, we added information about the relations between tables directly to the DBIC schema files. Once that was set up, we customized the `TTSite` View and created a page that listed all people and addresses in the database. Then, we created a Controller to edit, add, and delete people. The `edit` and `add` actions were simple forms, so we used `Catalyst::Controller::FormBuilder` to generate and validate the forms automatically. After this Controller was built, we created a similar one to add, edit, and update addresses, again using `FormBuilder` to generate the form HTML and JavaScript for us.

4
Expanding the Application

In this chapter, we will continue to work with our address book application and add some features that almost every application needs. We'll see how to move the configuration options out of application code and into an easy-to-maintain configuration file. We'll also learn how to search a database and create search results that span multiple pages. To bulk up our database so that searching is more meaningful, we'll write a script to import CSV files into the address book. We will also add sessions to our application, so that data can persist between requests. Finally, we'll explore authentication and authorization by implementing page-level and record-level access control.

Configuration files

The first new feature we'll add to our address book is the ability to be configured from an outside configuration file. This will allow us to easily change configurable aspects of our application without having to touch any of the application code. This is helpful during development, but really shines when a non-programmer (like an end user or a system administrator) needs to change a minor setting when the application is in production.

This feature will also be the easiest to add. Catalyst is set to read configuration from a file by default, and it creates an example configuration file in the application's main directory. In our case, the file is called `addressbook.conf`. This file is in the default configuration format and you can use other formats as mentioned in *Chapter 2, Creating a Catalyst Application*, if you choose to.

The simplest piece of configuration data you can add to your application is a single key-value pair (KVP). In YAML syntax, a configuration option `foo` set to `bar` will look like:

```
foo "bar"
```

Inside your application, you can access the value of `foo` via the `config` method in the application object:

```
print "Foo is: ". $c->config->{foo};
```

You can also configure individual components (Models, Views, and Controllers) from the `config` file by creating opening and closing tags. For example, the configuration for `MyApp::Model::MyDatabase` would be between the `<Model::MyDatabase>` and `</Model::MyDatabase>` tags. Setting the key `foo` to value `bar` inside `MyDatabase` would look like the following:

```
<Model::MyDatabase>
    foo "bar"
</Model::MyDatabase>
```

You can also configure directly inside the application class as follows:

```
package MyApp;
use Catalyst qw(...);
# ...
    __PACKAGE__->config('Model::MyDatabase' => { foo => 'bar' });
# ...
    __PACKAGE__->setup;
1;
```

To get at the form inside `Model::MyDatabase`, you can simply access a piece of class data with the name of the key as follows:

```
my_$foo = $self->{foo};
```

Though you can directly get the values of a configuration using the hash, it is always better to create an accessor, as follows:

Example:

```
package MyApp::Model::MyDatabase;
use parent 'Catalyst::Model';
  PACKAGE  ->mk_ro_accessors('foo');
sub chow_foo {
my $self = shift;
print "foo is equal to ". $self->foo;
}
```

In this example, we didn't need to access anything from a hash because Catalyst automatically created a (read-only) `accessor` method. The advantage of creating a method to access the data is that mistyping the name in your code somewhere will result in an error (instead of silently returning an undefined value). We also gain the ability to prevent writing, or perhaps return a default value if one isn't specified in the `config` file.

It is also possible to define Moose attributes in a Controller that can be set from the `config` file. These also allow for type constraints and value coercions. We will see more of this in Chapter 8.

Configuring the address book

At this point, our address book doesn't have many options to configure. However, there is one critical option, the location of the database. Looking inside `AddressBook::Model::AddressDB`, we can see that the database's location is hardcoded to the value that we initially specified. Fortunately, if we specify a database in the `config` file, it will override the hardcoded value. This means we don't have to modify any code to use a different database; we simply need to add the following option to our `addressbook.conf` file:

```
name AddressBook
<Model::AddressDB>
  connect_info dbi:mysql:__HOME__database
</Model::AddressDB>
```

The configuration information is an array of four elements. The first element is the DBI connection string. The second and third elements are the database username and password, respectively. The final element is a hash of configuration attributes to pass onto the database driver. `DBIx::Class` and Catalyst don't actually interpret this data, they just pass the array onto a `DBI->connect` call.

As SQLite doesn't use usernames or passwords, we haven't specified them in our configuration.

A configuration entry for a MySQL database (which does use usernames and passwords) would look similar to the following:

```
name AddressBook
<Model::AddressDB>
  connect_info dbi:SQLite:__HOME__database
  connect_info yourusernamefordb
  connect_info yourpasswordfordb
</Model::AddressDB>
```

More information on the connect configuration can be found at `http://search.cpan.org/~rkitover/Catalyst-Model-DBIC-Schema-0.40/lib/Catalyst/Model/DBIC/Schema.pm#connect_info`

The variable `__HOME__` is replaced with the path to the application by config loader.

Sessions

A feature that almost every web application needs is the ability to store application state for a certain user between requests. HTTP treats each request as being completely unrelated to every other request. This is usually undesirable in the context of a web application because some data needs to persist between page loads. For example, it would be very inconvenient to require a user to type his/her username and password on every page to authorize the next action. Sessions are the solution to this problem. When a user first visits your application, Catalyst will supply him/her with a token to identify himself/herself for a certain amount of time. Whenever that token is supplied with a request, Catalyst will find its session data and make it accessible in your Controllers throughout the request.

To get started with sessions, you'll need to install some modules and load the appropriate session plugins into your application. The modules we'll need to install are `Catalyst::Plugin::Session`, `Catalyst::Plugin::Session::State::Cookie`, and `Catalyst::Plugin::Session::Store::FastMmap` or `Catalyst::Plugin::Session::Store::File`.

Catalyst's session engine consists of three parts. The first is `Catalyst::Plugin::Session`, which provides general session functionality. For the session plugin to work, it needs to be able to do two things—store session data somewhere and be able to get a session ID token from each user. The most common form of a token is a cookie that's stored on the user's machine. When your application sets a cookie, the browser will store it and attach it to every request. Catalyst will see this cookie and then restore the appropriate session data. To use cookies to manage sessions, load `Catalyst::Plugin::Session::State::Cookie` into your application.

However, if the user's have disabled cookies for some reason, then this won't work. Nearly every browser and robot on the web today support cookies, so you shouldn't have to worry about browser support. If you absolutely cannot use cookies, try `Catalyst::Plugin::Session::State::URI`, but be aware that it can be buggy because it works by rewriting every link on your generated pages to include the session identifier in the URL. (It can also open up security issues. If a user follows a link to an external website, the external website will be able to retrieve the session ID from the `Referer` header and then steal the user's session. Therefore, it's recommended that you just use cookies.)

Once you have a way to identify each user, you'll need to store the data specific to the user somewhere. The most convenient method for this is `Catalyst::Plugin::Session::Store:: FastMmap`. `FastMmap` will store session data in a memory-mapped file, which is fast and efficient but won't be shared between load-balanced machines or persist between runs of your server.

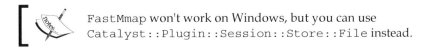 FastMmap won't work on Windows, but you can use
`Catalyst::Plugin::Session::Store::File` instead.

Storing the session data in your database will eliminate these problems, but it will
be slightly slower. Most real applications won't notice the speed difference. For
development, `Session::Store::File` and `Session::Store::FastMmap` are the
most convenient as they require no additional configuration.

After you've decided on which `Session::Store` and `Session::State` backends
to use, simply list them with the other plugins. Your `AddressBook.pm` should look
something like this:

```
use Catalyst qw/
    -Debug
    ConfigLoader
    Static::Simple
    Session
    Session::State::Cookie
    Scssion::Store::FastMmap
/;
```

When you restart your application, the first request will result in a cookie being
set. Each subsequent request with that cookie will be in the same session. You'll
also have access to a few new methods in your context object. The most useful are
`$c->session` and `$c->flash`. These methods both work like `$c->stash`, except they
persist for more than one request. Data stored with `$c->session` will persist until
the session expires (which you can check via the `$c->session_expires` accessor).
`$c->flash` is a little bit more complicated. It works like the stash, but will persist
between HTTP *redirects* (explained in detail later in this chapter). Once it's read or
written to after a redirect, it will be cleared out. The most convenient way of using
the flash is to set:

```
__PACKAGE__->config(session => {flash_to_stash => 1});
```

in `AddressBook.pm` with the rest of your configuration options. With this turned on,
the flash from the last request will automatically become the stash for the current
request. We'll see how this is helpful in the next section.

Adding sessions to the address book

Our address book doesn't need sessions in the traditional sense quite yet. It doesn't
need to store any data between requests, because nothing is specific to a single user.
Every user has the same privileges and every operation changes the data for every
other user. However, we can use sessions to improve the user interface.

In the version of AddressBook from *Chapter 3, Creating a Real Application* we programmed our mutator operations (/person/delete, for example) to set a message key in the stash and then forward back to the list action. This made deletes seamless—the user just clicked delete and then saw the updated list of people with a message at the top saying that the person had been successfully removed. The only problem was that the URL in the browser was still at /person/delete/number instead of /person/list. If a user bookmarked that URL assuming that it would lead them to the list of people, they could accidentally delete a person or just get an error message.

Catalyst will let us do better than that. To get the user's URL bar to show the real URL, we need to redirect him (via an HTTP redirection code) to the user list page. If we did that without sessions, everything in the stash would be lost and we wouldn't be able to display a status message at the top of the page. Thanks to the flash though, we can tell Catalyst to display the message on the next page load instead of the current page. All we need to do is enable flash_to_stash as done previously, store the message in $c->flash, and issue an HTTP redirect to the user list. Here's the code that implements this for the person deletion action in the person Controller (Person.pm):

```
sub delete : Local {
  my ($self, $c, $id) = @_;
  my $person = $c->model('AddressDB::People')->find({id => $id});
  $c->stash->{person} = $person;
  if($person){
    $c->flash->{message} = 'Deleted ' . $person->name;
    $person->delete;
  }
  else {
    $c->flash->{error} = "No person $id";
  }
  $c->response->redirect($c->uri_for_action('person/list'));
  $c->detach();
}
```

The only difference between this and the old code is that we are using the flash instead of the stash, and so we redirect instead of forward at the end.

The syntax for redirection might appear a bit confusing but it is really simple. Redirection works by setting a header in the HTTP response, and then sending the browser to another page. As the browser is outside the realm of Catalyst and doesn't know the full URL, we have to convert the name of the action to a real fully-qualified URL. We then set the necessary response header (`Location:`) to that URL. The `$c->detach()` line will stop all further processing of actions and jump directly to the end action. In this case, it's not strictly necessary (as the end action will be called immediately anyway), but if you're inside some if-then statements, `detach` will get you out as quickly as possible. After you `detach`, the default end action will see that this response is a redirect and will pass that on to the browser without rendering a template.

When the browser requests the `/person/list` page, Catalyst will restore the session, move the flash to the stash, and then handle the request as normal. (If this isn't working for you, make sure you enabled the `flash_to_stash` configuration option as described.) At the end of the request, the message from the flash will be displayed on top of the page, just like before. This all will be independent, so you won't have to change the templates at all.

Forwarding will continue to work as before, but you can gradually convert from forwarding to redirection as you see it. Now your users have the best of both worlds. They can bookmark any page and go to the right place, while still receiving informative status messages where necessary.

Sessions in the database

If you plan on deploying your application across multiple servers (via a load balancer), putting sessions in the database can make your life easier. You won't need to ensure that each user gets the same server for every request—everything will work perfectly even if the user moves between servers. This means that you can also take servers down without anyone losing data.

The setup isn't quite as simple as with `Session::Store::FastMmap` or `Session::Store::File`, but it is straightforward. The first thing to do is to create a `sessions` table in your database as follows:

```
CREATE TABLE sessions (
    id   CHAR(72)    PRIMARY KEY,
    session_data    TEXT,
    expires         INTEGER
);
```

Then, add a schema file, `lib/AddressBook/Schema/AddressDB/Session.pm` to your DBIC schema by recreating the Model as explained in the previous chapter.

```
$ perl script/addressbook_create.pl model AddressDB DBIC::Schema
AddressBook::Schema::AddressDB create=static dbi:SQLite:database
```

You will see something like the following:

```
exists "/Volumes/Home/Users/solar/Projects/CatalystBook/AddressBook/
script/../lib/AddressBook/Model"
 exists "/Volumes/Home/Users/solar/Projects/CatalystBook/AddressBook/
script/../t"
Dumping manual schema for AddressBook::Schema::AddressDB to directory /
Volumes/Home/Users/solar/Projects/CatalystBook/AddressBook/script/../lib
...
Schema dump completed.
 exists "/Volumes/Home/Users/solar/Projects/CatalystBook/AddressBook/
script/../lib/AddressBook/Model/AddressDB.pm"
```

Your changes in the other schema files are still intact provided you placed all the custom configurations below the following line in the schema:

```
# You can replace this text with custom content, and it will be
preserved on regeneration
```

The newly-created schema for the session will look like the following (`lib/Addressbook/Schema/AddressDB/Result/Sessions.pm`):

```
package AddressBook::Schema::AddressDB::Result::Sessions;
use strict;
use warnings;
use base 'DBIx::Class';
__PACKAGE__->load_components("InflateColumn::DateTime", "Core");
__PACKAGE__->table("sessions");
__PACKAGE__->add_columns(
  "id",
  { data_type => "CHAR", default_value => undef, is_nullable => 1,
size => 72 },
  "session_data",
  {
    data_type => "TEXT",
    default_value => undef,
    is_nullable => 1,
    size => undef,
  },
```

```
     "expiresinteger",
     { data_type => "", default_value => undef, is_nullable => 1, size =>
  undef },
  );
  __PACKAGE__->set_primary_key("id");
  # Created by DBIx::Class::Schema::Loader v0.04005 @ 2010-04-10
  14:20:53
  # DO NOT MODIFY THIS OR ANYTHING ABOVE! md5sum:wRNuyHfQA4yvyNDO6V9QEw
  # You can replace this text with custom content, and it will be
  preserved on regeneration
  1;
```

With the `Sessions` schema in place, all you have to do is use `Session::Store::DBIC` instead of `Session::Store::FastMmap` and add the following configuration option in `AddressBook.pm`:

```
  __PACKAGE__->config( session => {
    dbic_class => 'AddressDB::Session', flash_to_stash => 1 });
```

You will also have to install the plugin using CPAN and add it to the makefile (for portability) as explained in *Chapter 2, Creating a Catalyst Application*.

When you restart your application, session information will be stored in your DBIC model.

Using components from outside Catalyst

As you start using the address book, you might want to import and export data in a standard format. You could add a web interface for this functionality, but sometimes it's easier to just write a quick shell script to parse some outside data and enter it into our database. Thanks to the flexibility of Catalyst, scripts running outside of the main application can use the same Model (and even other components, if you can dream up a use for them) as the application and manipulate the database directly.

Using the `DBIx::Class` schema externally is pretty straightforward. All we need to do is use the `Schema`, connect to it, and add the data.

Let's write a script in the `script` directory that will accept lines of CSV-formatted data (for example, `firstname, lastname, Home, 123 Fake Street, 123-456-7890, address@example.com`) and add them to the database. We start our script by creating it in `script/import_csv.pl` and writing a bit of documentation:

```
  #!/usr/bin/env perl
  use strict;
  use warnings;
  =head1 NAME
```

```
import_csv.pl - imports CSV files into the address book
=head1 FORMAT
The data should be in CSV format with the following fields:
firstname, lastname, address location, address, phone, email
=cut
```

Next, we'll load the `Text::CSV_XS` module to parse the CSV data for us as follows:

```
use Text::CSV_XS;
```

Here's the tricky part:

```
use FindBin qw($Bin);
use Path::Class;
use lib dir($Bin, '..', 'lib')->stringify;
```

We want our application to work on any platform and be able to find the configuration file so that we can find the database automatically. We start by using the `FindBin` module to find the filename of our script (placed in the `$Bin` variable). As we put the script in `script/import_csv.pl` and our Catalyst application is rooted one level above, we use the `Path::Class` module to generate the filename of the `lib` directory that's one level above the location of our script. We use `Path::Class` instead of just writing `$Bin/../lib`, so that the script will run under operating systems other than UNIX. Once we have a filename, we pass it to the `lib` pragma to tell Perl to look for modules (our `Schema`) in that path.

Now we can safely load the schema and YAML to parse the `config` file:

```
use AddressBook::Schema::AddressDB;
use Config::JFDI;
use strict;
```

We are using `Config::JFDI` to load values from the configuration file. `Config::JFDI` replaces `__HOME__` with the relevant path just like `Catalyst::ConfigLoader`. For more details on this module, you can read `http://search.cpan.org/~rkrimen/Config-JFDI-0.064/lib/Config/JFDI.pm`.

```
my $filename = file($Bin, '..', 'addressbook.conf');
my $config = Config::JFDI->new(path => $filename);
my $dsn = $config->get->{'Model::AddressDB'}->{connect_info};
```

Our database's connection information in now in `$dsn`, and we can simply connect to the schema:

```
my $schema =
AddressBook::Schema::AddressDB->connect($dsn)
or die "Failed to connect to database at $dsn";
```

From there, everything works as it did inside our application, with a few caveats. Instead of using `$c->model('AddressDB::TableName')`, we write `$schema->resultset("TableName")`.

```
while(my $line = <>){
  eval {
    my $csv = Text::CSV_XS->new();
    $csv->parse($line) or die "Invalid data";
    my ($first, $last, $location, $address, $phone, $email)
    = $csv->fields();
    my $person = $schema->resultset('People')->
    find_or_create({ firstname => $first, lastname => $last,
    });
    $schema->resultset('Addresses')->
    create({ person => $person, location => $location, postal =>
$address,
        phone => $phone, email => $email,
    });
    print "Added @{[$person->name]}'s $location address.\n";
  };
  if($@){
    warn "Problem adding address: $@";
  }
}
```

The main loop is pretty simple. We first use `Text::CSV_XS` to parse the current line (STDIN or files specified on the command line) into the fields—first name, last name, location, postal address, phone number, and e-mail address. We then use the first name and last name to locate an entry in the `people` table (or create it if it doesn't exist). Then we use that `person` object to create an appropriate row in the `address` table, using the rest of the data. If that works, we print out a message saying that we added the user and then move on to the next line in the data file.

We also wrap the entire procedure in an `eval{}` block so that we can print an error message and move on to the next piece of data if there's an error.

There's one more thing we need to do before we can run this. The `find_or_create` method will only work if you guarantee to `DBIx::Class` that each `firstname` and `lastname` combination is unique (as we are using this constraint to add new addresses to the same person). We do this by creating a UNIQUE constraint in the database and then adding the following line to `AddressBook::Schema::Result::People`:

```
__PACKAGE__->add_unique_constraint(name =>
[qw/firstname lastname/]);
```

This tells `DBIx::Class` that the columns `firstname` and `lastname`, taken together, are unique (like a primary key). We name this constraint `name` so that we can distinguish between it and other constraints.

After you add that line to your schema, you should be able to run the application:

```
$ perl script/import_csv.pl
```

Test,Person,Home,123 **Home St.,123-456-7890,home@example.com**

Test,Person,Work,123 **Work ST.,890-123-4567,work@example.com**

^D

$

Now when we visit the website, we'll see a Test Person with a Work and Home address! As you can see, sometimes it's very convenient to access your application without a web interface. Some infrequent operations, like reporting or bulk imports, are easier to perform from the command line.

We'll conclude with a script to generate some random CSV data:

```perl
#!/usr/bin/perl
=head1 NAME
random_addresses.pl - generate random addresses
=head1 USAGE
Run like C<perl script/random_addresses.pl | perl script/import_csv.
pl>
=cut
my @names = qw(Foo Bar Baz Test Jonathan Rockway Person Another A);
my @locations = qw(Home Work Mobile Fax Test);
my @streets = qw(Green Oak Elm 60th Fake State Halsted);
for(1..200){
my $first = $names[rand @names];
my $last = $names[rand @names];
my $where = $locations[rand @locations];
my $number = int rand 9900 + 100; # 3-digit street number my $street
= $streets[rand @streets];
my $address = "$number $street St.";
my $phone = join '-', (int rand 800 + 100, int rand 899 + 100, int
rand 8999 + 1000);
my $email = "$first.$last\@$where.example.com";
print "$first,$last,$where,$address,$phone,$email\n";
}
```

Then we can run:

```
$ perl script/random_addresses.pl | perl script/import_csv.pl
```

When the last command finishes, you'll have 200 new addresses in your database—just in time for the next section on searching!

Thanks to the import script, our application now has all the power of the UNIX command line. Anything that can generate CSV data can now communicate with the application. (You can also try opening up the generated random addresses in your spreadsheet program; it should work fine.)

Searching and paging

Now that our application is starting to accumulate a significant quantity of data, it would be nice to be able to search it. In this section, we'll create an interface for searching addresses and names and displaying the search results. We'll start with a form for defining what the user wants to search for:

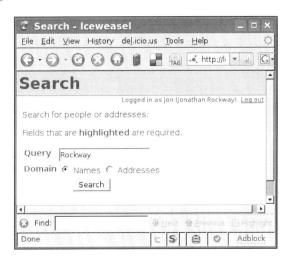

Then we'll search and display the results:

The first thing we'll do is create a Search Controller and then write the database logic for searching.

To do this, we'll create lib/AddressBook/Controller/Search.pm. We'll have a single action that will generate a search form and then display results when the form is submitted as follows:

```
package AddressBook::Controller::Search;
use Moose;
use namespace::autoclean;
BEGIN {extends 'Catalyst::Controller'; }
extends 'Catalyst::Controller::FormBuilder';
=head1 NAME
AddressBook::Controller::Search - Catalyst Controller
=head1 DESCRIPTION
Catalyst Controller.
=head1 METHODS
=cut
sub search : Global Form {
```

```
my ($self, $c, $query) = @_;
my $form = $self->formbuilder;
# get query from the URL (or the form if there's nothing there)
$query ||= $form->field('query') if ($form->submitted && $form-
>validate);
return unless $query;   # no query? we're done
$c->stash->{query} = $query;
my @tokens = split /\s+/, $query;
my $result;
if ('Names' eq $form->field('domain')) {
  $result = $c->forward('search_names', \@tokens);
  $c->stash->{'template'} = 'search/name_results.tt2'
}
else {
   $result = $c->forward('search_addresses', \@tokens);
   $c->stash->{'template'} = 'search/address_results.tt2' ;
}
my $page = $c->request->param('page');
$page = 1 if($page !~ /^\d+$/);
$result = $result->page($page);
$c->stash->{result} = $result;
my $pager  = $result->pager;
$c->stash->{pager} = $pager;
}
```

You can create the Controller using `script/addressbook.pl controller Search`
and update the code or simply create the file and fill it with the last code. It is not
necessary to use the helpers to create the Controller. They are merely helpers for
your convenience.

As mentioned in *Chapter 3, Building a Real Application* we will be
using `FormBuilder` in this example. If you are curious about HTML
`FormHandle` we will be using it in Chapter 8.

This is the bulk of the Controller. We start by getting a query string from the form or
the URL. If the form is empty, we halt further processing and redisplay the form.

If there is a search, we tokenize the search string by splitting the string into an array
of words. Our search is going to be a very simple search—it will look for any word
in any field. The search will also be limited to either names or addresses, not both.

In the next few lines, we determine whether the search domain is addresses or names and forward to a sub-action to actually do the search. When that action returns, we set the necessary template (name_results for the name search results, address_results otherwise).

Finally, we'll account for paging the results. Instead of displaying every result on one page, we'll split it up to show only 10 results per page. To do this, we simply call the page method on the resultset. Page will return a new resultset that will only contain 10 results. Also, if there's a numeric "page" parameter set in the URL, we'll skip to that page of the resultset ($page). Otherwise, we'll display the first page.

Lastly, we'll get a "pager" for this resultset. The pager is a Data::Page object and stores metadata about the paged resultset. It will allow us to easily create links to the first page of results, last page, next page, and previous page, and also contains the number of results on this page, the total number of results, the total number of pages, and so on. You could manually calculate these things, but it's tricky and time-consuming to get it right. Catalyst and DBIx::Class will handle all the tedious details of paging results automatically.

That's the bulk of our search. The next methods send the actual search requests to the database:

```perl
sub search_addresses : Private {
  my ($self, $c, @tokens) = @_;
  my @address_fields = qw/postal phone email location/;
  @address_fields     = cross(\@address_fields, \@tokens);
  return $c->model('AddressDB::Addresses')->
  search(\@address_fields);
}
sub search_names : Private {
  my ($self, $c, @tokens) = @_;
  my @people_fields = qw/firstname lastname/;
  @people_fields = cross(\@people_fields, \@tokens);
  return $c->model('AddressDB::People')->
  search(\@people_fields);
}
sub cross {
  my $columns = shift || []; my $tokens     = shift || []; map
{s/%/\\%/g}
    @$tokens;
  my@result;
  foreach my $column (@$columns){
    push@result,
    (map +{$column => {-like => "%$_%"}}, @$tokens);
  }
  return @result;
}
```

Most of the work is done in the `cross` subroutine, which generates a list of all columns paired with all the search tokens. As we're doing a text search, we want to use the `LIKE` predicate and enclose the terms in `%`. The SQL we want for a name search of "Test Person" is:

```
SELECT * FROM people WHERE firstname LIKE '%Test%' OR firstname LIKE
'%Person%' OR lastname LIKE '%Person%' OR lastname LIKE '%Test';
```

In `DBIx::Class` notation, we want:

```
$c->model('AddressDB::People')->
search([{ firstname => {-like => '%Test%'}},
{ firstname => {-like => '%Person%'}},
{ lastname => {-like => '%Test%'}},
{ lastname => {-like => '%Person%'}}]);
```

The `cross` routine simply returns the part that's inside of `search([])`.

Now that our logic is configured, we just need to generate the HTML. As with the forms in the last chapter, we'll use `FormBuilder` to automatically generate the search page. First, we'll create a `root/forms/search/search.fb` form as follows:

```
name: search
method: GET
header: 1
title: Search
fields:
  query:
  label: Query
  type: text
  required: 1
domain:
  label: Domain
  options: Names, Addresses
  required: 1
  submit: Search
```

We're using the `GET` method this time so that we can redo the search (via the results page) for each page. The first page will be at the URL `/search?query=Something`, the second page will be at `/search?query=Something&page=2`, and so on. We need the basic template to display this form as well:

```
[% META title="Search" %]
Search for people or addresses: [% FormBuilder.render %]
```

As you'd expect, that file lives in `root/src/search/search.tt2`.

The next thing to take care of is the results page. As the name results and address results pages are very similar, we're going to create a **wrapper** template that those two results will include. We'll just put it in `root/src/search/results_wrapper.tt2` so that we can include it in the real templates with minimum effort. Here's the code:

```
<h2>Search for [% query | html %]</h2>
<p>Displaying entries [% pager.first %]-[% pager.last %] of [%
  pager.total_entries %]
</p>
<ol start="[% pager.first %]"> [% content %]
</ol>
<hr /> Navigation:
&lt;&lt;
<a href="[% c.req.uri_with({ page => pager.first_page }) %]">First</a>
<a href="[% c.req.uri_with({ page => pager.previous_page
})%]">Previous</a>
|
<a href="[% c.req.uri_with({ page => pager.next_page })%]">Next</a>
<a href="[% c.req.uri_with({ page => pager.last_page }) %]">Last</a>
&gt;&gt;
or <a href="[% c.uri_for_action('/search/search') %]">Search again</a>
```

This template is actually where most of the interesting stuff happens. At the top, we use the `pager` object to provide some information about which page we're on, how many results there are, and so on. Then we start a numbered list at the first result on this page and include the content from the real template. After the real template (the template that actually displays the search results), we generate all the necessary navigation links. The key to this is the `$c->response->uri_with` (`[% Catalyst.res.uri_with( ... ) %]` inside the template) method. This method accepts a list of query string parameters (page in this case) and will replace the parameter with the provided replacement, keeping the rest of the URL the same as the current page. In this case, if we're at `http://localhost:3000/search?domain=Names&query=Some+Names+That+I+Like&page=8`, `[% Catalyst.res,uri_with({ page => 15 }) %]` would result in the URL `http://localhost:3000/search?domain=Names&query=Some+Names+That+I+Like&page=15`. This makes it very simple to modify the current URL—you don't need to parse anything.

We use `uri_with` four times, twice to generate the URLs for the first and last pages of the result, and twice to generate links to the next and previous pages of the results. A more polished application might want to hide the links for pages that don't exist (there's no next page when you're on the last page, for example). `Catalyst.uri_for_action` is similar to `Catalyst.uri` except that the former can handle change in `uri` for the same actions, for example, if you choose to have a uri listnew for the same action list (using `path` attribute). You will not have to change the code in `uri_for_action` as it is still referring to the `uri` for the same action (sub list).

For a more comprehensive list of methods available with the context object, read `http://search.cpan.org/~bobtfish/Catalyst-Runtime-5.80022/lib/Catalyst.pm`.

Now, we just need to create the two templates to display the results. We're going to copy the display logic from the template that displays the list of all people and their addresses. To make it easier to maintain our templates, we're going to extract the code that displays a single person and the code that displays a single address to separate templates. We'll then include that code from the `list.tt2` template, `name_results.tt2`, and `address_results.tt2`.

The first template will display an address stored in a variable called `address`:

```
<b>[% address.location | html %]</b>
<a href="[% c.uri_for_action('/address/edit',address.id) %]"> Edit</a>
<a href="[% c.uri_for_action('/address/delete',address.id) %]">
Delete</a>
<br />
<address>[% address.postal | html | html_line_break %]</address>
Phone: [% address.phone | html %]<br />
Email: [% address.email | html %]<br />
```

We'll store this in `root/src/address_fragment.tt2`, so it's clear that this is just a fragment of a page. Next is the `person_fragment.tt2` template, which will display a person (and his addresses) stored in a variable named `person`:

```
[% person.name | html %]
<a href="[% c.uri_for_action('/address/add',person.id) | html %]">Add
address</a>
<a href="[% c.uri_for_action('/person/edit',person.id) | html
%]">Edit</a>
<a href="[% c.uri_for_action('/person/delete',person.id) | html
  %]">Delete</a>
[% SET addresses = person.addresses %]
<ul>
  [% FOREACH address = addresses %]
  <li>[% INCLUDE address_fragment.tt2 %]</li> [% END %]
</ul>
```

Note that we're including the `address_fragment.tt2` template for every address that a person has. It's important to note that the `address` variable from this template will exist inside the template we include and that it's possible for the included templates to modify variables in the calling template. If you'd rather didn't want this to happen, use the `[% PROCESS %]` directive instead.

Let us modify root/src/person/list.tt2 to use the new fragments by replacing the existing WHILE loop with the following:

```
[% WHILE (person = people.next) %]
<li>[% INCLUDE person_fragment.tt2 %]</li> [% END %]
such that it looks like the following
[% META title = 'People' %]
[% IF people.count > 0 %]
<p>Here are people that I know about:</p>
<ul>
  [% WHILE (person = people.next) %]
  <li>[% INCLUDE person_fragment.tt2 %]</li> [% END %]
</ul>
[% ELSE %]
<p>No people yet!</p> [% END %]
<p> <a href="[% c.uri_for("/person/add") | html %]"> Add a new
person...
</a></p>
</li>
```

This cleans up the code quite nicely. We're finally ready to create the search results templates:

First, root/src/search/name_results.tt2:

```
[% META title = "Search results" %]
[% WRAPPER "search/results_wrapper.tt2" %] [% WHILE (person = result.
next) %]
<li>[% INCLUDE person_fragment.tt2 %]</li> [% END %]
[% END %]
```

Next, root/src/search/address_results.tt2:

```
[% META title = "Search results" %]
[% WRAPPER "search/results_wrapper.tt2" %]
[% WHILE (address = result.next) %]
<li>[% address.location | html %] address for [% address.person.name
%]<br />
[% INCLUDE address_fragment.tt2 %]
</li>
[% END %] [% END %]
```

Factoring templates into small fragments makes it very easy to modify something once and have it appear everywhere in your application. There's no code to cut and paste if you want the layout of both result pages to change. Just modify the wrapper and both pages will look the same.

Writing these templates was the final step to get the searching working. You should be able to start your application, navigate to /search, and search to your heart's content. If you need more data in your database, just run the import_csv.pl script again.

Authentication and authorization

Now that our application has some real data in it, it would be nice to show it only to the authorized users, not everyone on the Internet. In Catalyst, this is a two-step process. First, we use authentication plugins to determine who a user is. In the simplest case, we ask the user to enter a username and password. If the username is known and the password is correct, we assume that the person at the other end of the connection is the user whose username they specified. If we wanted to be more flexible, we could ask users to log in with **OpenID**, their Flickr username and password, or Bitcard. Either way, the end result is that we can authoritatively associate a username with the session and then act on that username to grant permission to restricted areas of our application. The granting of permission is the second stage — authorization.

Authentication

As with sessions, Catalyst handles authentication via an array of plugins. The main plugin is Catalyst::Plugin::Authentication. This plugin calls upon sub-plugins that handle the various details, such as reading the OpenID credentials or looking up a username and password in the database. Regardless of the plugins you use, you'll get a standard program interface. Every logged-in user gets a user object, accessible through $c->user->obj. If you use DBIC to store your usernames and passwords, then this object is a full DBIC resultset for the user's row in the user table. This will allow you to store user preferences in the database right next to their username and password, as well as create relations to other tables. Other backends might not put anything in the object, but the username will always be available via $c->user.

The simplest way to try authentication in your application is via the "Minimal" backend, with a setup like the following in your application's main file:

```
use Catalyst qw/
  -Debug
  ConfigLoader
  Static::Simple
  Session
  Session::State::Cookie
  Session::Store::DBIC
```

```
    Authentication
/; __
 __PACKAGE__->config( 'Plugin::Authentication' =>
    {
      default => {
        credential => {
          class => 'Password',
          password_field => 'password',
          password_type => 'clear'
        },
        store => {
          class => 'Minimal',
          users => {
            testuser1 => {
              password => "RanDo99",
              editor => 'yes',
              roles => [qw/edit delete/],
            },
          }
        }
      }
    }
  );
```

This will store usernames and passwords directly in the configuration file. This makes
testing very easy, as you can add any attributes to the user object by specifying keys
and values alongside the password or roles, without having to change your database
schema. Another easy way to get authentication going quickly is to generate an
Apache htpasswd file and use Authentication::Store::Htpasswd:

```
 __PACKAGE__->config( 'Plugin::Authentication' =>
    {
      default => {
        credential => {
          class => 'Password',
          password_field => 'password',
          password_type => 'clear'
        },
        store => {
          class => 'Htpasswd',
          file => '/path/to/passwd.file';
        }
      }
    }
  );
```

Once you have an authentication store and some users, you can create an action that reads the username and password from the user and calls `$c->authenticate({ username => $username, password => $password })`. If the username and password were correct, `$c->authenticate` will return `true` and store that fact in the session, so the user doesn't have to reauthenticate to every page. Once the user is logged in, your actions can test `$c->user` and act upon the information as they see it. When the user is done with his/her session, your application should call `$c->logout`, which will delete the session data. Later in the chapter, we will see how to use the DBIC to authenticate for the AddressBook application. More details on authentication can be found at `http://search.cpan.org/~flora/Catalyst-Plugin-Authentication-0.10016/lib/Catalyst/Plugin/Authentication.pm`.

Authorization

Having just a username isn't particularly useful, unless your application only wants to differentiate between logged-in users and anonymous users. If you'd like to apply different rules to different classes of users for different URLs, you'll want to use some of the Catalyst's authorization plugins.

The simplest authorization plugin is `Authorization::Roles`. This plugin provides methods for testing if a user belongs to a certain role or class of users. You'll need a backend that supports roles, but fortunately both the Minimal backend and the DBIC backend do. Using roles is very simple. At the beginning of your action, you call `$c->assert_user_roles(qw/role1 role2/)`. This method will throw an exception unless the user is a member of both `role1` and `role2`. For example, an action called `edit_management_reports` might look like this:

```
sub edit_management_reports {
  my ($self, $c) = @_;
  $c->assert_user_roles(qw/manager editor/);
  generate_reports();
}
```

Unless a user is both a manager and an editor, the `generate_reports()` command will never be called. The user will instead get an *access denied* error message.

`$c->assert_user_role(qw/role1 role2/)` works similarly, but only requires a user to possess one (not all) of the mentioned roles. If you want more control over what happens when a user is denied access, you can use `$c->check_user_role(s)` instead. These methods work like `assert_user_role(s)`, but return `true` if the check succeeds and return `false` otherwise. You can check the result in an `if` statement, and act accordingly:

```
if($c->check_user_role(qw|administrator editor|)){
  do_the_edit();
}
else {
  $c->stash->{error} = "You are not authorized to edit this.";
  $c->detach('/denied');
}
```

This is the most basic way to use roles to control access. A more flexible option is the `Authorization::ACL` plugin. This plugin allows you to set up per path rules that are tested on each request. If all of the checks pass, the user is allowed to access the page. Otherwise, an `/access_denied` method is executed instead. This method can display an error to the user, or check some other credentials and allow access anyway.

For example, to use the ACL to disallow access to `/admin` for non-administrators, your `MyApp.pm` (or `AddressBook.pm`) file will look like the following:

```
use Catalyst qw/ConfigLoader Static::Simple
Session Session::State::Cookie Session::Store::DBIC Authentication
Authorization::Roles
Authorization::ACL/;
# setup sessions, authorization, and authentication
## ACL rules
  __PACKAGE__->deny_access_unless('/admin', [qw/admin/]);
```

This code will check the user's role on every request to `/admin`. If the user isn't in all of the listed roles (only 'admin' in this case), then the request goes to `/access_denied` instead of `/admin`. This rule will also apply to `/admin/list/user/123` and anything in a path below `/admin`.

If you prefer not to use roles, you can also use an arbitrary subroutine:

```
  __PACKAGE__->allow_access_if(
    '/bonus/area',
    sub { my ($c, $action) = @_;
      if($c->user->karma > 50){
        return $ALLOWED;
      }
```

```
    else {
      return $DENIED;
    }
  }
);
```

Here we allow access to `/bonus/area` only if the user has a karma (as defined by the user object) greater than 50. Otherwise, the `/access_denied` action is run instead. Note that in this example we have written a custom method that returns `true` or `false` based on some condition, which is then used as an input for `allow_access_if`.

Also, being able to define rules for ACL using `__PACKAGE__` allows easy application of arbitrary rules to an entire portion of the application, without having to change any Controller code.

Adding authentication and authorization to the address book

Now that we've had an overview of authentication and authorization, let's restrict access to our address book. To make the management of users and roles as easy as possible, we'll store the user data and role data in our DBIC Model. For now, we'll manually add users to the database and set their usernames and passwords. We'll also optionally associate an entry in the `person` table with each user, to allow non-editors to edit their own addresses. Finally, we'll create two roles, "viewer" and "editor" and restrict access to the site via an ACL. We'll let viewers view any data and allow editors to mutate that data (edit/create/delete). Also, we'll make an exception—if a user is a viewer but wants to add or delete his own addresses, we'll allow that.

The first step is to create the necessary tables in our database as follows:

```
$ sqlite3 database
CREATE TABLE user (id INTEGER PRIMARY KEY, username TEXT, password TEXT,
person INTEGER);
INSERT INTO user VALUES(1, 'edit', 'editme', 1); INSERT INTO user
VALUES(2, 'view', 'viewme', 2); CREATE TABLE role (
  id INTEGER PRIMARY KEY,
  role TEXT
);
```

```
INSERT INTO role VALUES(1, 'editor'); INSERT INTO role VALUES(2,
'viewer'); CREATE TABLE user_role (
  user INTEGER REFERENCES user, role INTEGER REFERENCES role,
  PRIMARY KEY (user, role)
);
INSERT INTO user_role VALUES(1, 1); INSERT INTO user_role VALUES(1, 2);
INSERT INTO user_role VALUES(2, 2);
DELETE FROM people; -- Clear out the database INSERT INTO people
VALUES(1, 'Editor', 'Person'); INSERT INTO people VALUES(2, 'Viewer',
'Person');
```

Here, we created three tables, a `user` table to store username, passwords, and the link to the `people` table; a `role` table to store a list of roles; and a `user_role` table to apply roles to each user. Then we added two users, "edit" and "view" with passwords "editme" and "viewme" respectively.

> We're using cleartext passwords for testing. When we deploy the application, we'll encrypt the password so that the passwords are not revealed if the database is stolen.

We also added "editor" and "viewer" roles and made "edit" a member of the "editor" and "viewer" role, and "view" only a "viewer". Finally, we created the entries in the `people` table for each user.

Next, we'll use the Catalyst helper script to create the new schema as follows:

```
script/addressbook_create.pl model AddressDB DBIC::Schema AddressBook::
Schema::AddressDB create=static dbi:SQLite:database
```

Notice that this should have created three new schema files, `Role.pm`, `User.pm`, and `UserRole.pm`. Note that the helper has already determined the relationship between `role` and `user_role`. We will edit `User.pm` to add the relationship with `user_role` and `people`.

Make sure the three schema look like the following:

```
User.pm
package AddressBook::Schema::AddressDB::Result::User;
use strict;
use warnings;
use base 'DBIx::Class';
__PACKAGE__->load_components("InflateColumn::DateTime", "Core");
__PACKAGE__->table("user");
__PACKAGE__->add_columns(
  "id",
  {
```

```
    data_type => "INTEGER",
    default_value => undef,
    is_nullable => 1,
    size => undef,
  },
  "username",
  {
    data_type => "TEXT",
    default_value => undef,
    is_nullable => 1,
    size => undef,
  },
  "password",
  {
    data_type => "TEXT",
    default_value => undef,
    is_nullable => 1,
    size => undef,
  },
  "person",
  {
    data_type => "INTEGER",
    default_value => undef,
    is_nullable => 1,
    size => undef,
  },
);
__PACKAGE__->set_primary_key("id");
# Created by DBIx::Class::Schema::Loader v0.04005 @ 2010-04-14
20:54:46
# DO NOT MODIFY THIS OR ANYTHING ABOVE! md5sum:0WYaHOZ/ZNIE1tU7qd3k3A
# You can replace this text with custom content, and it will be
preserved on regeneration
__PACKAGE__->has_many(map_user_role => 'AddressBook::Schema::
AddressDB::Result::UserRole', 'user');
__PACKAGE__->belongs_to(person => 'AddressBook::Schema::AddressDB::
Result::People');
__PACKAGE__->many_to_many( roles => 'map_user_role', 'role' );
1;


Role.pm
package AddressBook::Schema::AddressDB::Result::Role;
use strict;
use warnings;
use base 'DBIx::Class';
```

```
  __PACKAGE__->load_components("InflateColumn::DateTime", "Core");
  __PACKAGE__->table("role");
  __PACKAGE__->add_columns(
    "id",
    {
      data_type => "INTEGER",
      default_value => undef,
      is_nullable => 1,
      size => undef,
    },
    "role",
    {
      data_type => "TEXT",
      default_value => undef,
      is_nullable => 1,
      size => undef,
    },
  );
  __PACKAGE__->set_primary_key("id");
  # Created by DBIx::Class::Schema::Loader v0.04005 @ 2010-04-14
  20:54:46
  # DO NOT MODIFY THIS OR ANYTHING ABOVE! md5sum:h20Spzb/nmESWeqFwzqJUg
  # You can replace this text with custom content, and it will be
  preserved on regeneration
  __PACKAGE__->has_many(map_user_role => 'AddressBook::Schema::
  AddressDB::Result::UserRole', 'role');
  1;


  UserRole.pm
  package AddressBook::Schema::AddressDB::Result::UserRole;
  use strict;
  use warnings;
  use base 'DBIx::Class';
  __PACKAGE__->load_components("InflateColumn::DateTime", "Core");
  __PACKAGE__->table("user_role");
  __PACKAGE__->add_columns(
    "user",
    {
      data_type => "INTEGER",
      default_value => undef,
      is_nullable => 1,
      size => undef,
    },
    "role",
```

```
      {
        data_type => "INTEGER",
        default_value => undef,
        is_nullable => 1,
        size => undef,
      },
  );
  __PACKAGE__->set_primary_key("user", "role");
  # Created by DBIx::Class::Schema::Loader v0.04005 @ 2010-04-14
  20:54:46
  # DO NOT MODIFY THIS OR ANYTHING ABOVE! md5sum:fibVKCta/8LNK7VleF0OGQ
  __PACKAGE__->belongs_to(user => 'AddressBook::Schema::AddressDB::
  Result::User', 'user');
  __PACKAGE__->belongs_to(role => 'AddressBook::Schema::AddressDB::
  Result::Role', 'role');
  # You can replace this text with custom content, and it will be
  preserved on regeneration
  1;
```

You may notice that we have added custom relationships in the schema file. Following is the explanation of the syntax and usage of these relationships:

- **Has_many**: In this relationship, the package in which this is defined has a primary key that is accessed by the foreign class. In our example, we have a has_many relationship in `User` and `Role` class, as the ID of both these classes are primary keys in `UserRole`. The first argument to this relationship is the relationship name, the second is the related classes, and the third is the field in the foreign class that acts as foreign key. The third argument can also be a condition.

- **Belongs_to**: This relationship is complimentary to has_many. It is defined in the class that is referring to another class's primary key. In this example, belongs_to is defined in the `UserRole`. As in has_many, the first argument is the relationship name and the second is the name of the foreign class. The third argument can optionally be the field in class that will refer to the foreign class or a condition.

- **Many_to_Many**: This relationship is simple and consists of two has_many relationships. The first argument is the name of the relationship. As many_to_many is just two has_many relationships, the second and third arguments are merely the names of the two has_many relationships.

For more information on relationships in `DBIx::Class` you may want to refer to `http://search.cpan.org/~frew/DBIx-Class-0.08121/lib/DBIx/Class/Relationship.pm`.

Now we just need to configure the application to use these schemata in
`AddressBook.pm` as follows:

```
__PACKAGE__->config( name => 'AddressBook' );
__PACKAGE__->config( session => {
        dbic_class => 'AddressDB::Sessions',
        expires => 3600,
        flash_to_stash => 1,
    }
);
__PACKAGE__->config->{'Plugin::Authentication'} =
  {
  default => {
    store => {
      class => 'DBIx::Class',
      user_class => 'AddressDB::User',
      password_type => 'clear', # use salted_hash for real
applications
      role_relation => 'roles',
      role_field => 'role'
    },
    credential => {
      class => 'Password',
    }
  }
  };
# Start the application
__PACKAGE__->setup();
```

Now our application is set to use authentication information from the database and
we're ready to start implementing the guts of our authentication infrastructure. Note
that we have used the name of the many_to_many relationship we just set up as the
value for `role_relation`, and the belongs_to relationship name from `UserRole`
for `role_field`.

Now, we need to create `login`, `logout`, and `access_denied` method. It is a good
practice to place these in a separate Controller as follows:

```
Perl script/addressbook_create.pl controller Auth
Auth.pm (lib/AddressBook/Controller/Auth.pm)
package AddressBook::Controller::Auth;
use Moose;
use namespace::autoclean;
BEGIN {extends 'Catalyst::Controller'; }
extends 'Catalyst::Controller::FormBuilder';
```

```
=head1 NAME
AddressBook::Controller::Auth - Catalyst Controller
=head1 DESCRIPTION
Catalyst Controller.
=head1 METHODS
=cut
sub access_denied : Private {
  my ($self, $c) = @_;
  $c->stash->{template} = 'denied.tt2';
}
sub login : Global Form {
  my ($self, $c) = @_;
  my $form = $self->formbuilder;
  return unless $form->submitted && $form->validate;
  if ($c->authenticate( {username => $form->field('username') ,
password =>
     $form->field('password')} ))
  {
    $c->flash->{message} = 'Logged in successfully.';
    $c->res->redirect($c->uri_for('/'));
    $c->detach();
  }
  else {
    $c->stash->{error} = 'Login failed.';
  }
}
sub logout : Global {
  my ($self, $c) = @_;
  $c->logout;
  $c->flash->{message} = 'Logged out.';
  $c->res->redirect($c->uri_for('/'));
}
=head1 AUTHOR
Antano Solar John
=head1 LICENSE
This library is free software. You can redistribute it and/or modify
it under the same terms as Perl itself.
=cut
#__PACKAGE__->meta->make_immutable;
1;
```

These three actions are very simple. `access_denied` just displays the access denied template when the user isn't authorized to access a certain page. `logout` calls `$c->logout` and redirects the user to the main page, with a message saying that the logout has succeeded. Finally, `login` reads in a `FormBuilder` form and checks the provided username and password. If it matches a user database, the login succeeds. If it doesn't match, we let the user try again, while displaying an error message on top of the login form, as shown in the following screenshot:

Notice the use of `Global` attribute. As mentioned in *Chapter 3, Building a Real Application* this allows us to call the `login` action with the `/login` URI instead of `/auth/login`.

The login form and login template go in the usual places, `root/forms/auth/login.fb` for the form definition and `root/src/auth/login.tt2` for the template, and are very similar to the forms and templates we've already created:

Login.tt2:

```
[% META title="Log in" %] [% FormBuilder.render %]

login.fb
  name: login
  method: POST
  header: 1
  title: Login
fields:
  username:
```

```
    label: username
    type: text
    required: 1
  password:
    label: password
    type: password
    required: 1
    submit: Login
```

We'll also modify our global header in `root/lib/site/layout` to show the logged-in user's name:

```
<div id="header">[% PROCESS site/header %]</div>
<div id="userinfo">
[% IF c.user %]
Logged in as  [% c.user.username %]    ([% c.user.person.name %])
<a href="[% c.uri_for('/logout') %]">Log out</a>. [% ELSE %]
Not logged in. <a href="[% c.uri_for('/login') %]">Log in</a>.
[% END %]
</div>
<div id="content">
  [% IF error %]
<p><span class="error">[% error | html %]</span></p> [% END %]
[% IF message %]
<p><span class="message">[% message | html %]</span></p> [% END %]
  [% content %]
</div>
<div id="footer">[% PROCESS site/footer %]</div>
```

Note that the first and last lines should already exist in the file. We'll also need to update the CSS (`root/src/ttsite.css`) a bit, so that the username displays in a small font on the right side of the screen:

```
#userinfo {
  font-size: .8em;
  text-align: right;
}
```

On restarting the server, you should be able to visit /login, type in a username and password and be logged in! Clicking the logout link should cause Catalyst to forget that you logged in (and allow you to log in again). With that working, we're ready to add the final feature—*authorization*.

We'll implement authorization in two stages. First, we'll add generic rules to only allow viewers to view pages that contain address data. To the end of AddressBook.pm, after __PACKAGE__->setup(), add the following:

```
## ACLs
  __PACKAGE__ ->deny_access_unless('/person', [qw/viewer/]);
  __PACKAGE__ ->deny_access_unless('/search', [qw/viewer/]);
  __PACKAGE__ ->deny_access_unless('/address', [qw/viewer/]);
# should always be allowed
  __PACKAGE__ ->allow_access('/index');
  __PACKAGE__ ->allow_access('/login');
```

We'll also need the template to display when the user is denied access, root/src/denied.tt2:

```
[% META title="Access denied" %]
[% IF !error %]You are not allowed to access this resource.[% END %]
[% IF !c.user %]
<a href="[% c.uri_for_action('/auth/login') %]">Logging in</a> might
help. [% END %]
```

This template does a few different things. If the user is not logged in, then the page suggests that the user should authenticate and then try again. If an error message has been specified, then that's displayed. Otherwise, a default message is displayed: *You are not allowed to access this resource.*

The final step is to add a rule to all edit actions to see if a user is a member of the editor role or if she/he is editing his own entry. So, at the top of each editing action, add some code like the following:

```
# check ACL
$address = $c->model('AddressDB::Address')->...
if($c->user->person)
{
  if($address->person->id != $c->user->person->id &&
     !$c->check_any_user_role('editor')){
       $c->stash->{error} =
      'You are not authorized to edit or delete addresses for this
person.';
       $c->detach('/auth/access_denied');
     }
  }
  else
  {
    $c->stash->{error} = 'No Person attached to your login!';
    $c->detach('/person/list');
  }
```

You'll want to add this to the edit and delete actions in `AddressBook::Controller::Person` and `AddressBook::Controller::Address`, modifying the error message as appropriate. You also might want to disallow a user from deleting his/her name, as that will cause the foreign key in the `user` table to dangle into nowhere.

When you've made those changes, fire up the application and explore the robust access control system that you've created!

 When planning ACL for your application, it is neater to have private actions or Controller methods that get called with the roles and error message as arguments.

You may also want to read `http://wiki.catalystframework.org/wiki/gettingstarted/howtos/interim_authorization_and_authentication_example`.

Summary

In this chapter, we added some of the most common features that web applications need to our address book application. We learned how to make deployment easy by using the configuration file. Next, we saw how to store data between requests with Session plugins, and how to use Session plugin to make the user's experience more consistent and enjoyable. We also learned how to identify users and use their identity to control access to the application. Later, we programmed search logic and learned how to display resultsets that span multiple pages. Finally, we learned how to utilize our application's model outside of our application.

5
Building a More Advanced Application

In this chapter, we'll build a brand new application from scratch while exploring the advanced features of Catalyst, DBIx::Class, and the Template Toolkit. We'll start by modeling our data and building a DBIx::Class schema. Then we'll add some extra code to the schema to abstract some more complex queries. After that we'll build a web interface to the database with just a few lines of code. Finally, we'll add some editing features to the web interface. In the course of this chapter, you will also be learning some nice ways to debug including interactive shell. In the end, you will also learn a powerful feature called chaining dispatcher that allows for a certain kind of abstraction with Controller methods.

The application

The application we'll be building in this chapter is called **ChatStat** and arises from a need to track the opinions of irc.perl.org denizens. A common convention on irc.perl.org is to add ++ or -- and a quip after a word. These one-liners are usually amusing and deserve to live on after they've scrolled off the screen. So, we'll write a Catalyst application to make this data available on the Web.

Following is a glimpse of what you are going to build:

- Best/worst/most controversial and least controversial topic listing:

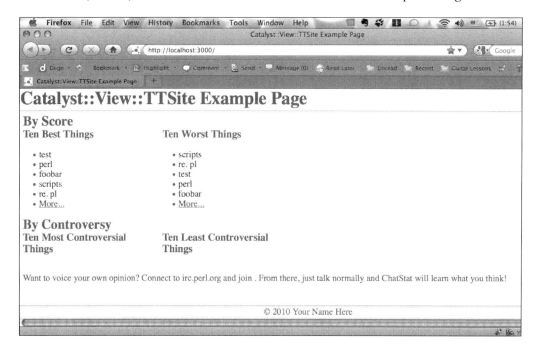

- Reasons for being loved and hated for a single item:

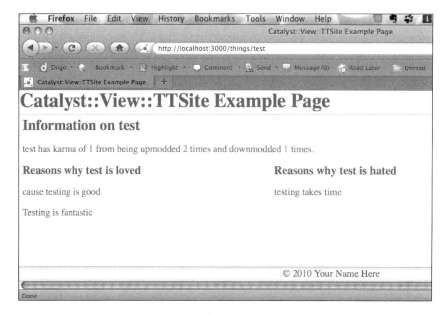

- Reasons for ups and downs (chained actions just like the previous):

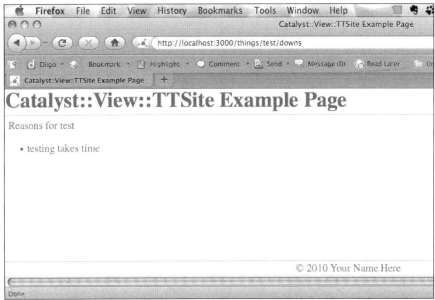

Background

Before we set up the data model, it's important to understand what data we need to keep track of. The most important piece of data to track is the actual opinions from the IRC channel. A complete opinion on IRC looks something like the following:

```
(on #channel) < nickname> (some thing)++ # things are good
```

Here we see nickname saying that he likes some thing on #channel because things are good. In our database, we'll want to store each opinion as a parsed entity consisting of columns for the channel, the nickname, the thing ("some thing" here), how many points were given (1 for "++", 0 for "+-", and -1 for "--"), the comment ("things are good"), and finally the entire message (so that we can fix up the other columns if we find our parser not working properly later).

For the sake of making queries easier to write, we'll also normalize the data. This means that there will be a `things` table that gives each thing a unique ID and similar tables for the `nicknames` and `channels`. This will result in an `opinions` table that has records like "57, 42, 89, 6, 1, 'message', and 'something++ # message'". 57 is the (opinion) primary key, 42 is the nickname primary key, 89 is the thing primary key, 6 is the channel, and so on. Database management systems work best with this sort of data (as redundancy is eliminated) and it makes it easy to add metadata to the entities later. (A nickname will consist of a hostname, username, and nickname; a channel will consist of an IRC network and channel names, and so on.) Normalizing the data means that it's simple to add extra metadata later, without affecting the existing queries.

Finally, as one person (in real life) can have multiple nicknames, we'll add a `person` table to group related nicknames together. Each nickname will belong to one person.

Creating the database

First, we'll create the application so that we have some place to put our database file. We won't be doing much with Catalyst to start, but we'll need the project eventually:

```
$ catalyst.pl ChatStat
$ cd ChatStat
```

Let's get started by creating the tables in SQLite as follows:

```
$ sqlite3 root/database
CREATE TABLE channels (
  cid INTEGER PRIMARY KEY NOT NULL, channel TEXT NOT NULL
);
```

```
CREATE TABLE nicknames (
  nid INTEGER PRIMARY KEY NOT NULL, pid INTEGER NOT NULL,
  nick TEXT NOT NULL, username TEXT NOT NULL, host TEXT NOT NULL
);
CREATE TABLE opinions (
  oid INTEGER PRIMARY KEY NOT NULL, nid INTEGER NOT NULL,
  cid INTEGER NOT NULL, tid INTEGER NOT NULL, message TEXT NOT NULL,
  reason TEXT NOT NULL, points INTEGER NOT NULL
);
CREATE TABLE people (
  pid INTEGER PRIMARY KEY NOT NULL, name TEXT NOT NULL
);
CREATE TABLE things (
  tid INTEGER PRIMARY KEY NOT NULL, thing TEXT NOT NULL
);
CREATE UNIQUE INDEX channel_channels on channels (channel);
CREATE UNIQUE INDEX hostmask_nicknames on nicknames (nick, username,
  host);
CREATE UNIQUE INDEX nickname_people on people (name);
CREATE UNIQUE INDEX thing_things on things (thing);
CREATE INDEX idx_opinions_tid ON opinions (tid);
```

The tables are pretty straightforward, but note that we are creating some unique indices for various columns. This ensures that we can't accidentally give a thing multiple ID numbers and end up with a useless opinions table. It also makes writing the database code easier; we can look up a thing by its name instead of its unique ID (primary key), as the database guarantees that each thing will only appear in the things table once. The hostmask_nicknames index is a bit different; the data we get from IRC is in the form (nick, username, and host) so that the index will let us retrieve the unique ID given to that data.

Finally, we have a regular index on opinions.tid. We'll be grouping by this column in many queries, so it's logical to index. Doing so reduces the runtime of some queries from two seconds per query to thirty or more queries per second!

Now that we have the tables in place, we'll need to generate a DBIx::Class schema and add the relationships:

```
$ perl script/chatstat_create.pl model DBIC DBIC::Schema ChatStat::Schema
create=static dbi:SQLite:root/database
```

This will create the files in `lib/ChatStat/Schema/Result/*`. Let us look at those files one at a time and add the constraints.

First, let us look at `People.pm`. All we need to add here is a name for our unique constraint.

Here's the constraint:

```
__Package__   ->add_unique_constraint(
  nickname => [qw/name/]
);
```

This will allow us to write the following:

```
my $jrockway = $people->find('jrockway',
  { key => 'nickname' });
```

Later in the application, it's ensured that a UNIQUE INDEX over name will be created when we redeploy the schema.

Here's the has_many relationship:

```
__Package__   ->has_many( "nicknames", "ChatStat::Schema::Nicknames",
  { "foreign.pid" => "self.pid" },
);
```

This command will tell `DBIx::Class` to create an accessor called `nicknames` that will return an array of `ChatStat::Schema::Nickname` objects. The third argument is the join condition specified in `SQL::Abstract` syntax. In this case, we say to join on `people.pid = nicknames.pid`. For more information on `SQL::Abstract` syntax you can read `http://search.cpan.org/~frew/SQL-Abstract-1.65/lib/SQL/Abstract.pm`.

`Nicknames.pm` will look similar. We have another unique constraint, a has_many relationship to `opinions` (every nickname has many opinions), and a belongs_to relationship back to `People`. The belongs_to relationship will allow us to access the `person` record when we have only a nickname.

Here's the code:

```
__Package__   ->add_unique_constraint(
  hostmask => [qw/nick username host/]
);
__Package__   ->has_many( "opinions", "ChatStat::Schema::Opinions",
  { "foreign.nid" => "self.nid" },
);
__Package__   ->belongs_to( "person","ChatStat::Schema::People",
  { pid => "pid" }
);
```

The has_many relationship looks the same as the one we just created.

The belongs_to relationship is also similar. We say to create a `person` accessor that will return a `ChatStat::Schema::People` object for the person. We've also abbreviated the join condition here, omitting the reference to foreign and self because foreign and self are implied automatically when they're omitted and there are no other conditions. It saves a bit of typing.

Moving along, let's take a look at the `Things.pm` file. We're going to add another unique constraint and has_many relationship here:

```
__Package__    ->add_unique_constraint(
  thing => [qw/thing/]
);
__Package__    ->has_many( "opinions", "ChatStat::Schema::Opinions",
  { "foreign.tid" => "self.tid" },
);
```

By now this pattern should be looking familiar. The has_many relationship will create an `opinions` accessor that will return a list of opinions that relate to the current "thing".

`Channels.pm` is going to look almost exactly the same:

```
__Package__    ->add_unique_constraint(
  channel => [qw/channel/]
);
__Package__    ->has_many( "opinions", "ChatStat::Schema::Opinions",
  { "foreign.cid" => "self.cid" },
);
```

Finally, we'll edit `Opinions.pm` and add belongs_to relationships to compliment the has_many relationships we just created:

```
__Package__    ->belongs_to( "nickname", "ChatStat::Schema::Nicknames",
  { nid => "nid" },
);

__Package__    ->belongs_to( "thing", "ChatStat::Schema::Things",
  { tid => "tid" },
);
__Package__    ->belongs_to( "channel", "ChatStat::Schema::Channels",
{ cid => "cid" },
);
```

That's all we need to do. Now every piece of data is related properly, allowing us to get whatever data is needed in a Perl fashion. Setting up a normalized schema is a bit more work, but the data is more organized and working with it using DBIx::Class will be a pleasure.

Populating the database

An empty database isn't much fun, so let's add some data to it. In the version of this application that I use, I have a POE-based IRCBot dynamically adding data to the database as messages come in from IRC. As POE is beyond the scope of this book, we'll create a small command-line script that works similarly. For the curious, the IRCBot code is included with the book and lives under the ChatStat::Robot namespace.

For the data-adding script, we'll take the same approach as the IRCBot. We'll start with a string that looks like an IRC message, parse it into its components, and then add it to the database.

Let us start with a class to abstract the components of the message. In lib/ChatStat/Action.pm, create the following:

```
package ChatStat::Action;
use strict;
use warnings;
use Regexp::Common qw/balanced/;
use base 'Class::Accessor';
__Package__  ->mk_accessors(qw|who channel word points reason
  message|);
use Readonly;
Readonly my %OP_POINTS => ( '++' => 1,
                           '--' => -1,
                           '-+' => 0,
                           '+-' => 0,
                         );
sub new {
  my ($class, $who, $where, $what) = @_;
  my $self = $class->SUPER::new({ who => $who, channel => $where,
    message => $what
  });
  $self->_parse;
  return $self;
}

sub _parse {
  my $self = shift;
```

```
    my $what = $self->message;
    my $parens = $RE{balanced}{-parens=>'(){}[]<>'}{-keep};
    if ($what =~ /
        (?:                          # what we're voting on:
          $parens                    # something in parens
          |   #  -or-
          ([A-Za-z_:0-9]+)           # a single word++
        )
        ([+-]{2})                    # the operation (inc or dec)
          \s*                        # spaces, who cares
        (?:[#] \s* (.+)$)?           # and an optional reason
          /x
        )
    {
      my $paren = $1;
      my $word = $2;
      if (defined $paren) {
        $paren =~ s/^[({[<]//;
        $paren =~ s/[)}\]>]$//;
        $word = $paren;
      }
      my $op = $3;
      my $reason = $4;
      $reason = '' if !defined $reason;
      # trim
      $word =~ s/^\s+//;
      $word =~ s/\s+$//;
      $reason =~ s/^\s+//;
      $reason =~ s/\s+$//;
      # it worked
      $self->word(lc $word);
      $self->reason(lc $reason);
      $self->points($OP_POINTS{$op} || 0);
      return;
    }
    die 'parse error';
  }
1;
```

Note that this class is not really a Catalyst application. We are using it to merely populate our database.

This class takes a nickname, channel name, and message, and sets up a data structure consisting of the parsed out parts. For example, when you invoke:

```
my $a = ChatStat::Action->new('jon', '#test',
'Catalyst++ # fun');
```

You'll be able to access the components like the following:

```
my $nick = $a->who;           # jon
my $points = $a->points;      # 1 (-1 if we said --)
my $reason = $a->reason;      # fun
my $word = $a->word;          # catalyst
```

We use `Regexp::Common` to parse out balanced sets of parentheses so that we can add points to a phrase like "a phrase" by typing "(a phrase) ++". Thanks to `Regexp::Common::balanced`, we can use any paired brackets we want, like `<something>++` or `{something else}--`.

With the parsing out of the way, we want to be able to add one of these actions to the database. Because of the normalized schema, we have to do some extra work. We need to create the dependencies of the opinion first (thing, nickname, and channel) and then insert the actual opinion record. The nickname object is created similarly as it needs to refer to an existing person object.

As there's a lot to do, let's add a subroutine to the schema (in `lib/ChatStat/ResultSet/Schema.pm`) called `record`, which will insert an action object into the database as follows:

```
sub record {
  my $self = shift;
  my $action = shift;
  my $nickname = $self->_get_nickname(action->who);
  my $thing = $self->resultset('Things')->
  find_or_create({ thing => $action->word });
  my $channel = $self->resultset('Channels')->
  find_or_create({ channel => $action->channel });
  return $self->resultset('Opinions')->
  create({ nickname => $nickname,
           thing => $thing,
           points => $action->points,
           message => $action->message,
           reason => $action->reason,
           channel => $channel,
        });
}
```

All we do here is use the DBIC schema (`$self`) to create or find the relevant records, then we create an `Opinion`. We do need a `_get_nickname` subroutine to take the nickname (in the form of `nickname!~username@hostname.com`, and return a nickname object that refers to a (perhaps newly-created) `person` object:

```
sub _get_nickname {
  my $self = shift;
  my $fullid = shift;
  my ($nick, $user, $host) = ($1, $2, $3) if  $fullid =~
  m/(.*)!~(.*)@(.*)/ig;
  my $nickname = $self->resultset('Nicknames')->find_or_new({ nick =>
    $nick, username => $user, host => $host,});
  my $person = $nickname->person;
  if (!$person) {
  my $person = $self->resultset('People')->find_or_create({ name =>
    $nick });
  $nickname->person($person);
}
$nickname->update_or_insert;
return $nickname;
}
```

Now we can get an `Action` and put it into the database with one line of code:

```
$schema->record(ChatStat::Action->new(...));
```

Let's tie this all together by creating a script in `script/chatstat_add_opinion.pl` so that we can add opinions from the command line as follows:

```
use strict;
use warnings;
use FindBin qw($Bin);
use lib "$Bin/../lib";
use ChatStat::Action;
use ChatStat::Schema;
my ($channel, $who, $message) = @ARGV;
die 'need channel as arg 1' unless $channel;
die 'need nickname as arg 2' unless $who;
die 'need message as arg 3' unless $message;
my $s = ChatStat::Schema->connect("DBI:SQLite:$Bin/../root/database");
die "failed to connect to database" unless $s;
my $parsed = ChatStat::Action->new($channel, $who, $message);
my $new = $s->record($parsed);
print "added opinion ". $new->oid. "\n";
```

You can now run this using the following command line:

```
$ perl script/chatstat_add_opinion.pl 'jon!~jon@jrock.us' '#foo'
'scripts++ # making my life easy'

added opinion 1
```

Extracting the data

Now that our database is full of data, it's time to make some sense out of it. We'll start by writing a function to determine the total number of points a "thing" has accumulated.

Instead of writing a script to test each query we write, we'll use a **read-evaluate-print loop (REPL)** to interact with our program in real time. To get a Perl REPL, install the Devel::REPL module from CPAN. That module provides a script called re.pl. Run re.pl, and you'll be able to type in Perl code as though you're at a shell prompt that understands Perl.

As an example, let us try adding an opinion from re.pl:

```
$ re.pl # the > is now re.pl's prompt
> use lib qw(lib);
> use ChatStat::Action;
> use ChatStat::Schema;
> my $s = ChatStat::Schema->connect('DBI:SQLite:root/database');
$ChatStat_Schema1 = ChatStat::Schema=HASH(0x8aafda0);
> my $a = ChatStat::Action->new('jon!~jon@jrock.us', '#test', '(re.
    pl)++');
$ChatStat_Action1 = ChatStat::Action=HASH(0x90dbe40);
> $a->message; (re.pl)++
> $a->reason;
> $a->points;
1
> my $o = $s->record($a);
$ChatStat_Schema_Opinions1 = ChatStat::Schema::Opinions=HASH(0x915a450);
> $o->id;
6
> $o->nickname->person->name;
jon
> exit
```

If you want to explore your program or you're only going to do something once or twice, re.pl is a great way to do it. You can write a script to use repl and make the schema connection available for you. For example, the following script when placed in the script folder can read the configuration from the model file and make a $s available for you that refers to the schema:

Script/chatstat_repl.pl

```
use Devel::REPL;
my $repl = Devel::REPL->new;
$repl->load_plugin('LexEnv');
$repl->lexical_environment->do(<<'CODEZ');
use FindBin;
use lib "$FindBin::Bin/../lib";
use ChatStat::Model::DBIC;
use ChatStat::Action;
my $schema_class = 'ChatStat::Schema';
my $dsn = 'dbi:SQLite:root/database',
eval "use $schema_class";
my $s = $schema_class->connect($dsn);
CODEZ
$repl->run;
```

Save this script in script/chatstat_repl.pl. We will use it later for debugging.

Back to the task at hand, let's write a function to return the number of points a thing has accumulated. For now, we'll add this function to the thing Opinions resultset:

lib/ChatStat/Schema/ResultSet/Opinions.pm

```
package ChatStat::Schema::ResultSet::Opinions;
use base 'DBIx::Class::ResultSet';

sub karma_for {
  my $self = shift;
  my $thing = shift;
  my $dir = shift;
  my @points;
  if (defined $dir && $dir == -1) {
    @points = ('points' => {'<=', -1});
  }
  elsif (defined $dir && $dir == 1) {
    @points = ('points' => {'>=', 1});
  }
  elsif (defined $dir && $dir == 0) {
    @points = ('points' => {'==', 0});
```

```
  }
  my $col = $self->search({ 'thing.thing' => lc $thing, @points, },
                          { join => ['thing'], })->get_column('points');
  if (defined $dir) {
    return $col->func('count');
  }
  return $col->sum || 0;
}
1;
```

We're introducing few new features of DBIx::Class here. We start with a straightforward search of the opinions table, looking for rows where thing.thing equals the $thing passed into the function. However, there is no column called thing.thing in the opinions table. To get that, we want to join along the "thing" relationship we created earlier. This is what the second argument search does; we pass a list of relationships to join in as "join", and now the columns in the related table are available to use in the search query. (If you want to get back the value of a joined in column, specify include_columns => [qw/table.list table.of table.columns/] after join.)

At this point, we have a resultset. When we call get_column on that resultset, an object representing a single column of the resultset is returned. The object has methods such as sum to return the sum of everything in that column, all to return an array of values, and so on. We call sum to sum up the points, and then return that sum.

The critical thing to keep in mind is that even though we call methods and create objects, no query goes out to the database until we ask for a result. This means that get_column isn't actually getting the column from the database and converting it to a Perl array; it merely sets a flag saying we only need to get this column when we actually run the query. When we say $col->sum at the end, that tells DBIx::Class to execute the query; the sum command is done on the database side with the SQL function SUM.

We can explore the actual SQL that this command generates by setting the environment variable DBIC_TRACE=1 and then running karma_for:

```
$ DBIC_TRACE=1 script/chatstat_repl.pl
> $s->karma_for('catalyst');
SELECT SUM( points ) FROM opinions me  JOIN things thing ON ( thing.tid =
me.tid ) WHERE ( thing.thing = ? ): 'catalyst'
2
> exit
```

You can see that the generated SQL is pretty efficient and probably what you would have written yourself.

Let's take the `karma_for` subroutine a bit further and add an option to only count the karma that goes in a certain direction (the sum of all upvotes, the sum of all downvotes, and so on).

To do this, we just need to add another condition to the search (limiting the selection to rows where points are less than zero, greater than zero, and so on). We add this to the top of `karma_for`:

```
my $dir = shift;
my @points;
if (defined $dir && $dir == -1) {
  @points = ('points' => {'<=', -1});
}
elsif (defined $dir && $dir == 1) {
  @points = ('points' => {'>=', 1});
}
elsif (defined $dir && $dir == 0) {
  @points = ('points' => {'==', 0});
}
Then we pass @points to search:
search({ 'thing.thing' => lc $thing,
  @points,
},
```

Finally, if `$dir` was passed in, we will want to call the COUNT function instead of the SUM function, so we add the following condition for that before we return the sum:

```
if (defined $dir) {
  return $col->func('count');
}
```

Back in `re.pl`, we can try out the new functionality:

```
> $s->karma_for('catalyst', -1);
SELECT COUNT( points ) FROM opinions me  JOIN things thing ON ( thing.tid
= me.tid ) WHERE ( points <= ? AND thing.thing = ? ): '-1', 'catalyst'
0
> $s->karma_for('catalyst');
SELECT SUM( points ) FROM opinions me  JOIN things thing ON ( thing.tid =
me.tid ) WHERE ( thing.thing = ? ): 'catalyst'
2
```

Chained resultsets

The most powerful abstraction DBIx::Class provides is the **resultset**. Every query you create with DBIx::Class is a resultset, and a new resultset can be created by chaining a resultset command off of an existing resultset. As an example, let's use script/chatstat_repl.pl (and resultset chaining) to find a list of people that have shared their opinions on the same things I have. Let us add some sample data as follows:

```
> $s->resultset('Opinions')->delete; # clear out opinions
> $s->record(ChatStat::Action->new('jon!~a@a','a','test++'))
> $s->record(ChatStat::Action->new('jon!~a@b','a','perl++'))
> $s->record(ChatStat::Action->new('foo!~c@c','c','test++'))
> $s->record(ChatStat::Action->new('bar!~d@d','c','test--'))
> $s->record(ChatStat::Action->new('quux!~q@q','q','foobar++'))
```

Now, we'll find jon as follows:

```
> my $me = $s->resultset('People')->find('jon', { key => 'nickname' })
> $me->name jon
```

And the nicknames he's used as follows:

```
> $me->nicknames
$ARRAY1 = [ ... ];
> map { $_->host } $me->nicknames
$ARRAY1 = ['a', 'b'];
```

This tells us that jon has used IRC from hosts a and b, which is exactly what we just typed.

Now, let's find opinions that those nicknames have authored:

```
> my $opinions = $me->nicknames->search_related('opinions')
> map { $_->oid } $opinions->all
$ARRAY1 = [1, 2]
```

Now we can join in the things that these opinions refer to using the following command line:

```
> my $things = $opinions->search_related('thing');
> $things->get_column('thing')->all
$ARRAY1 = [ 'test', 'perl' ];
```

Now for the fun part—we join everything back in reverse. We get the opinions that refer to these things, then we join in the nicknames that authored those opinions, then we find the person that those nicknames belong to:

```
> $things->search_related('opinions')
->search_related('nickname')
->search_related('person', {}, {group_by => 'person.name'})
->get_column('name')->all;
$ARRAY1 = [ 'bar', 'foo', 'jon' ];
```

To avoid duplicates at the last step, we added a GROUP BY clause to the query so that we would only see a person's name once.

Let's take this one step further and only show people who upmodded things that jon had an opinion about:

```
> $things->search_related('opinions',{'opinions_2.points'=>
{'>', 0}})
->search_related('nickname')
->search_related('person', {}, {group_by => 'person.name'})
->get_column('name')->all;
$ARRAY1 = [ 'foo', 'jon' ];
```

In this final query, bar went away because he only downmodded test, and that opinion was filtered out by the search passed to the first search_related call. Note that if a table is visited twice along the chain, it's referred to the second time by <tablename>_2 instead of just the table name. (This scales as high as you'd like it to.) If you're curious, the final generated SQL statement was as follows:

```
SELECT name FROM nicknames me LEFT JOIN opinions opinions ON (
  opinions.nid = me.nid )
JOIN things thing ON ( thing.tid = opinions. tid ) LEFT JOIN opinions
  opinions_2 ON ( opinions_2.tid = thing.tid)
JOIN nicknames nickname ON ( nickname.nid = opinions_2.nid )
JOIN people person ON ( person.pid = nickname.pid ) WHERE ( ( ( opinions_
2.points >= ? ) AND ( me.pid = ? ) ) ) GROUP BY person.name
```

As you can see, even though we stored intermediate results to named variables, the final query is run only once and no filtering of the results is done in Perl. Due to this, even complicated queries don't take a speed hit; they run the same as if you had executed the SQL yourself.

One last thing to note is that you need not end the chained resultset with get_column or all; you can use any method you would use on a normal resultset (including another search).

Custom resultsets

As the complexity of your queries increases, you might want to start giving them names so that you can use them like the other resultset methods. You can easily do this by adding a method to a package that extends the resultset. To extend the methods on the People.pm schema, you will create People.pm in lib/ChatStat/Schema/ResultSet/People.pm.

Note that the definition of the People schema is in lib/ChatStat/Schema/Result/People.pm and any extension to the methods can be called on a resultset in lib/ChatStat/Schema/ResultSet/People.pm.

In People resultset (lib/Schema/ResultSet/People.pm) add the following:

```
package ChatStat::Schema::ResultSet::People;
use base 'DBIx::Class::ResultSet';
sub similar_people {
my $rs = shift;
return $rs
->search_related('nicknames')
->search_related('opinions')
->search_related('thing')
->search_related('opinions')
->search_related('nickname')
->search_related('person', {}, {group_by => 'person.name'});
}
```

Now we can use the similar_people as a resultset method as follows:

```
my @similar = $people->search(...)->similar_people
->get_column('names')->all;
```

The normal accessor methods that are created in a schema class may return resultsets, but they won't be called from a resultset. So, if you want similar_people to work on the result of $people->find(...), it should be in a package that extends the resultset and not in the schema.

Putting the data on the Web

Now that we have the database set up, we're ready to build a web interface. We will present a summary of the data we collect and provide links for getting more information.

The main page, pictured below, is where we'll start. It displays the results of two queries (highest/lowest score and most/least controversial). The items themselves are links to pages that show the reasons each voter provided for upvoting or downvoting the thing.

Let us start by creating some macros that will make writing the actual pages much easier. Every time we see a "thing", we want it to be a link to the things page. Similarly, we always want negative scores to show up in red, and positive scores in green. Finally, we want nicknames to be linked to that person's information page. To make this easy to achieve, we'll write some common macros and include those on each page. Then, we can use the syntax [% score(some_ score) %] to format our data consistently.

The macros for score, thing, and person can be placed in root/src/thing_macros.tt2, and should look like the following:

```
[% # format a thing %]
[% MACRO thing(thing) BLOCK %]
<a class="thing"
href="[% c.uri_for('/things',thing) | html%]"> [% thing | html %]</a>
[% END %]


[% # format a person's nickname %]
[% MACRO person(person) BLOCK %]
<a class="person"
href="[% c.uri_for('/people',person) | html%]"> [% person | html %]</a>
[% END %]


[% # format a score %]
[% MACRO score(score) BLOCK %] [% IF score > 0 %]
[% SET class = "positive" %] [% ELSE %]
[% SET class = "negative" %] [% END %]
<span class="[% class %]_score"> [% score | html %]
</span>
[% END %]
```

As our application display results in two columns, let us create template root/src/pair.tt2 to do this:

```
<div class="pair clearfix" [% IF width %] style="width: [% width %]"
[% END %]>
<h2>[% title | html %]</h2>
<div class="box left">
  <h3>[% left_title | html %]</h3> [% left %]
</div>
<div class="box right">
  <h3>[% right_title | html %]</h3> [% right %]
</div>
<br class="clear" />
</div>
```

We can use this elsewhere like the following:

```
[% INCLUDE pair.tt2 title='Pair Title'
  left_title = 'The left side'
  left = 'some HTML for the left side' right_title = 'Ten right side'
  right = 'some HTML for the right side
%]
```

Before we write the main page, we just need a macro that will format a list of the thing-score list from the database into HTML, which can then be passed to `pair.tt2` as left and right. As we will use this on more than just the main page, we'll put the macro in `thing_macros.tt2` with the other macros:

```
[% # transform a list of [thing, score] list into HTML %] [% MACRO
  list_things(key,more) BLOCK %]
  <ul>
    [% FOREACH row = key %]
    <li>
      [% thing(row.thing) %]
      [% score(row.total_points) %]
    </li>
    [% END %]
    [% IF more %]
    <li><a href="[% more | html %]">More...</a></li> [% END %]
  </ul>
[% END %]
```

Now we're ready to write the main page, root/src/index.tt2:

```
[% PROCESS thing_macros.tt2 %]
[% MACRO list_controversy(rs) BLOCK %]
<ul>
[% FOREACH row IN rs %]
<li>[% thing(row.thing) %] [% score(row.total_points) %] (<span
  class="positive_score">[% row.ups | html%]</span>
  <span class="negative_score">[% row.downs | html %]</span>)
</li>
[% END %]
</ul>
[% END %]
[% INCLUDE pair.tt2 title='By Score'
  left_title = 'Ten Best Things'
  left = list_things(top_ten,c.uri('/things'))
  right_title = 'Ten Worst Things'
  right = list_things(bottom_ten,c.uri_for('/things'))
%]
```

```
[% INCLUDE pair.tt2 title='By Controversy'
  left_title = 'Ten Most Controversial Things' left =
    list_controversy(most_controversial)
  right_title = 'Ten Least Controversial Things' right =
    list_controversy(least_controversial)
%]
<p>Want to voice your own opinion?  Connect to irc.perl.org and join
[% channels | html %].  From there, just talk normally and ChatStat
will learn what you think!  </p>
```

We start including the macros. We use PROCESS instead of INCLUDE so that the macros are treated as though they were actually typed inside main.tt2. INCLUDE will throw them away after the included template is processed. We continue by defining a macro to format the controversy data, as it differs slightly from the best/worst data. After that we're ready to show our two pairs (best/worst and the controversy), and a bit of explanatory text.

Now, we need to actually get this data from the database into the template. We'll start with the Root Controller in lib/ChatStat/Controller/Root.pm:

```
package ChatStat::Controller::Root;
use Moose;
use namespace::autoclean;
BEGIN { extends 'Catalyst::Controller' }
#
# Sets the actions in this controller to be registered with no prefix
# so they function identically to actions created in MyApp.pm
#
__PACKAGE__->config(namespace => '');
=head1 NAME
ChatStat::Controller::Root - Root Controller for ChatStat
=head1 DESCRIPTION
 [enter your description here]
=head1 METHODS
=head2 Main
The Main page (/)
=cut
sub main : Path Args(0) {
  my ($self, $c, @args) = @_;
  $c->stash(template => 'index.tt2');
  # highest/lowest by score
  $c->stash(top_ten=> [$c->model('DBIC::Things')->highest_rated]);
  $c->stash(bottom_ten=>[$c->model('DBIC::Things')->lowest_rated ]);
  # controversy
```

```
    $c->stash(most_controversial => [$c->model('DBIC::Things')
      ->most_controversial]);
    $c->stash(least_controversial => [$c->model('DBIC::Things')
    ->least_controversial]);
    # list of joined channels
    my @channels = @{$c->config->{bot}{channels}||[]};
    my $last = pop @channels if @channels > 1;
    my $channels = join ', ', @channels;
    $channels .= " or $last" if $last;
    $c->stash(channels => $channels);
}
=head2 default
Standard 404 error page
=cut
sub default :Path {
    my ( $self, $c ) = @_;
    $c->response->body( 'Page not found' );
    $c->response->status(404);
}
=head2 end
Attempt to render a view, if needed.
=cut
sub end : ActionClass('RenderView') {}
=head1 AUTHOR
Antano Solar John
=head1 LICENSE
This library is free software. You can redistribute it and/or modify
it under the same terms as Perl itself.
=cut
__PACKAGE__->meta->make_immutable;

1;
```

All we do here is call some custom resultset methods (`highest_rated`, `lowest_rated`, `most_controversial`, and `least_controversial`) that we will define in `ChatStat::Schema::ResultSet:Things`. We also get a list of IRC channels from the `config` file (`$c->config`) and join those so that users looking at the page know where to go to vote for things.

The final step is to write those custom resultset methods as follows in `lib/ChatStat/Schema/ResultSet/Things.pm`:

```
=head2 highest_rated([$how_many [, $multiplier]])
Returns a resultset page of C<$how_many> highest rated items, or 10 if
not specified.  If C<$multiplier> is C<-1>, then the lowest-rated
items are returned instead.  (C<$multiplier> defaults to 1.)
my @top_ten = $schema->resultset('Opinions')->highest_rated();
```

```
my @bot_ten = $schema->resultset('Opinions')->highest_rated(10, -1);
my @top_40  = $schema->resultset('Opinions')->highest_rated(40);
...
From there:
my $first = @top_ten[0];
say $first->thing->thing. ' has '. $first->total_points. ' points';
=cut
sub highest_rated :ResultSet {
my $self  = shift;
my $count = shift || 10;
my $mult  = shift || 1;
croak "bad multiplier $mult; use 1 or -1" if $mult != -1 && $mult !=
1;
my $sort = $mult > 0 ? 'DESC' : 'ASC';
return $self->search({},
{ '+select' => [{ SUM => 'opinions.points'}],
  '+as'  => [qw/total_points/],
  join  => ['opinions'], group_by  => 'me.tid',
  order_by  => "SUM(opinions.points) $sort",
  rows  => $count,
  page  => 1,
});
}
=head2 lowest_rated([$how_many])
Abbreviation for highest_rated($how_many, -1)
=cut
sub lowest_rated :ResultSet {
shift->highest_rated(shift(), -1);
}
```

lowest_rated is just an alias for highest_rated, but sorted backwards.
highest_rated is where all of the real work happens. The top part of the function
reads the arguments, translates 1 or -1 into DESC or ASC sort order, and supplies
values for optional arguments. The real meat is the call to search. The empty {}
passed means that we don't want to constrain the results at all; we want every row
in the things table. The next hash reference is a list of modifiers. +select says to
select additional columns, specified as an array reference. Here, we're selecting SUM
(opinions.points). We can use opinions as we passed it as an argument to the
join attribute. Note that opinions is the name of the DBIx::Class relationship, not
the name of the table. The +as we pass gives the SUM (opinions.points) a name,
total_points, that we can pass to get_column to get the value. For convenience,
we should create an accessor to get this for us:

```
sub total_points {
my $self = shift;
# if we've joined this in, use the version we already have my
```

```
$fast = eval { $self->get_column('total_points') };
return $fast if defined $fast;
# if it's not there, compute it with another SQL query return

$self->opinions->get_column('points')->sum;
}
```

This accessor first looks to see if we already have `total_points`, and if we do, returns it. If we don't ask for `total_points` when we do the query, it will be calculated separately.

 if you're going to call `total_points` on every row, it's best to join it in like we do in `highest_rated`. If you don't, every call will result in a trip to the database, requiring a new query for every single row.

We have seen the other attributes passed to search in the `highest_rated` string. `order_by` defines the sort order (like SQL's ORDER BY keyword) and `group_by` will set the grouping for aggregates, in this case the `tid` column in `opinions`. Rows and page set up paging; we usually want 10 rows and the first page, so we pass 10 and 1 to each of those attributes.

With that in place, the first half of our main page loads. Now we just need the controversy data. Here are `least_controversial` and `most_controversial` in `lib/ChatStat/Schema/ResultSet/Things.pm`:

```
sub most_controversial {
  my $self  = shift;
  my $count = shift;
  my $algo = '-(ABS(SUM(points))+COUNT(1))/(COUNT(1)+0.1)';
  $self->_controversial($count, $algo, 'DESC');
}
sub least_controversial {
  my $self  = shift;
  my $count = shift;
  my $algo = '-ABS(SUM(points))/(COUNT(1)+0.8)';
  $self->_controversial($count, $algo, 'ASC');
}
```

These methods simply set up the SQL for determining the controversy and pass it to the `_controversial` function, which does the real work. The basic idea is that the most controversial items have scores close to zero because they've been upmodded and downmodded an equal number of times. The least controversial items have high scores with little opposition.

Here's `_controversial`, which does the real work:

```
sub _controversial {
  my $self  = shift;
  my $count = shift || 10;
  my $algo  = shift;
  my $order = shift;
  $algo .= ' co';
  return
  $self->search({},
    { '+select' => [ \$algo,
      { SUM => 'points'},
      \'ABS(SUM((POINTS+1)/2))',
      \'ABS(SUM((POINTS-1)/2))',
      { COUNT => 1 },
     ],
    '+as'  => [qw/controversy total_points ups downs c/],
    join   => ['opinions'],
    group_by => 'me.tid',
    order_by => "co $order",
    having  => "COUNT(1) > 5",
    rows   => $count,
    page   => 1,
   });
}
```

What we do here is select the controversy rating ($algo), the total score, the number of upmods, the number of downmods, and the total count of upmods and downmods (for ordering). We introduce a new attribute, `having`, which is the same as SQL's HAVING clause.

Now we have everything we need to run the application. If you start the application, you should be able to visit the main page and see the highest rated things, lowest rated things, most controversial things, and least controversial things. Of course, remember to create the View with `script/chatstat_create.pl view TT TTSite`.

You must now be able to run the server `script/chatstat_server.pl` and open `http://localhost:3000` in a browser to see a page like the following:

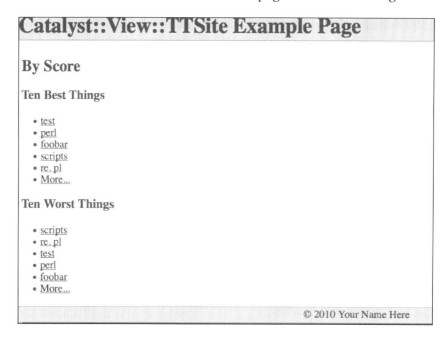

Some of the common errors that you may encounter are as follows:

- Missing 1; at the end of the newly-created resultset files (`lib/ChatStat/Schema/ResultSet/Things.pm` and `lib/ChatStat/Schema/ResultSet/People.pm`)

- Creation of the `tt2` files outside of `src` directory

All that's missing is formatting, which you can improve by modifying `root/src/ttsite` to contain the following:

```
* {
    background-color: white;
}

h2 { margin: 0 }
span.positive_score {
  color: green;
}
span.negative_score {
  color: red;
}
a.thing {
```

```
    color: black;
    text-decoration: none;
}
.pair {
    width: 30em;
}
.pair h3 {
    margin: 0;
    padding: 0;
}
.box   {
    width: 47%;
}
.pair .left   {
    float: left;
}
.pair .right {
    float: right;
}
.clearfix:after { content: "."; display: block;
    height: 0px; clear: both; visibility: hidden;
}
#logos {
  padding-top: 2em;
}
#logos img {
  border: none;
}
html {
  height: 100%;
}

body {
  background-color: [% site.col.page %];
  color: [% site.col.text %];
  margin: 0px;
  padding: 0px;
  height: 100%;
}
#header {
  background-color: [% site.col.head %];
  border-bottom: 1px solid [% site.col.line %];
}
```

```
#footer {
  background-color: [% site.col.head %];
  text-align: center;
  border-top: 1px solid [% site.col.line %];
  position: absolute;
  bottom: 0;
  left: 0px;
  width: 100%;
  padding: 4px;
}
#content {
  padding: 10px;
}

h1.title {
  padding: 4px;
  margin: 0px;
}

.message {
  color: [% site.col.message %];
}

.error {
  color: [% site.col.error %];
}
```

Now you can reload and see everything neatly laid out.

Notice that though it is advisable to use uri_for_action for every link, we have used uri_for, as uri_for will not throw an error even if action does not exist yet. It is important for us to check the progress of the site at every stage. It may be a good idea to replace uri_for with uri_for_action after the completion of the site.

At this point, we're ready to start making some of the links work. We'll start with the More... link, which shows a list of everything in the database.

Let's start by adding a resultset that will return everything and its score to lib/ChatStat/Schema/ResultSet/Things.pm:

```
sub everything {
  my $self  = shift;
  return $self->search({},
  { '+select' => { SUM =>
    'opinions.points' },
```

```
        '+as' => 'total_points',
        join => 'opinions',
        group_by => 'opinions.tid',
    });
}
```

This is simple compared to the queries we wrote before. We're simply selecting everything and adding the total points to the results.

 This query is actually a superset of the queries we wrote previously. As resultsets can be chained, it's possible to write the other queries as a search chained off of this one.

With this `everything` query, let's move on to writing the Controller. We'll need to create a new one, `Perl script/chatstat.pl create controller Things`, and replace the `index` method to look like the following (`lib/ChatStat/Controller/Things.pm`):

```
sub all_things :Path Args(0) {
    my ($self, $c) = @_;
    $c->stash(template => 'things.tt2');
    $c->stash(everything => [
    $c->model('DBIC::Things')->
    everything->search({},{ order_by =>
    'SUM(opinions.points) DESC'})
    ]);
}
```

Here we get a list of everything with our `everything` resultset method, and then filter it further, so it's sorted according to the number of points. Notice how we are chaining search on the resultset from the `everything` method.

Finally, we need a template, `root/src/things.tt2`, to display this data:

```
<h2>Every Thing</h2>
[% PROCESS thing_macros.tt2 %] [% FOREACH row = everything %]
<p>[% thing(row.thing) %] [% score(row.total_points) %]</p> [% END %]
```

Writing the template becomes pretty simple when all the macros are set up for you in advance.

Now we're ready to write the most interesting page in the application, the "thing" overview page. On this page, we'll be able to see the karma for the item, the number of upmods and downmods, and all of the written opinions. Here's what the page will look like:

As we already have most of the data we need for this page, let's start by writing the Controller. Below the `all_things` method we just wrote, add a `one_thing` method as follows:

```
sub one_thing :Path Args(1) {
  my ($self, $c, $thing) = @_;
  my $o = $c->model('DBIC::Opinions');
  my $m = $c->model('DBIC');
  # Aggregates
  $c->stash(template => "thing.tt2");
  $c->stash(thing => $thing);
  $c->stash(points => $o->karma_for($thing));
  $c->stash(ups => $o->karma_for($thing, 1));
  $c->stash(downs => $o->karma_for($thing, -1));
  $c->stash(person => $m->resultset('People')->find({ name =>
    $thing}, { key => 'nickname' })
  );
  # detailed reasons
  my @reasons = $c->model('DBIC::Things')->reasons_for($thing);
  my @up_r = grep { $_->points >    0 } @reasons; my @dn_r = grep {
    $_->points < 0 } @reasons; my @nu_r = grep { $_->points == 0 }
  @reasons;
  $c->stash(up_reasons => \@up_r);
  $c->stash(down_reasons => \@dn_r);
  $c->stash(neutral_reasons => \@nu_r);
}
```

Note that this action accepts one argument (the thing), so that it is `:Path Args(1)` instead of `:Path Args(0)`.

We do have a few queries in this action. We get the karma for the thing, and the number of ups and downs it received. We also look for a person with the same nickname as the thing and pass it to the template if there is one. Finally, we get all the textual reasons for these things, and sort them into upmod reasons, downmod reasons, and neutral reasons.

Here's the code (in `/lib/ChatStat/Schema/ResultSet/Things.pm`) for reasons_for:

```
sub reasons_for {
  my $self = shift;
  my $thing = shift;
  return $self->
  search({ thing => $thing })->
  search_related(opinions => {reason => {'<>' => q{}}});
}
```

This method returns all the opinions that are related to this thing, that have a non-NULL (or empty) textual reason.

The template for this action, `root/src/thing.tt2`, is straightforward as follows:

```
[% PROCESS thing_macros.tt2 %]
[% MACRO list_reasons(opinions) BLOCK %] [% FOREACH opinion =
  opinions %]
<div class="reason">
  <p><span class="opinion_reason">[% opinion.reason | html %]</span>
    <span class="written_by">[% person(opinion.person) %]</span>
  </p>
</div>
[% END %]
[% IF opinions.size < 1 %] <p>None!</p> [% END %] [% END %]
<h2>Information on [% c.stash.thing | html %]</h2>
<p>[% c.stash.thing | html %] has karma of [% score(points) %] from
  being upmodded [% score(ups) %] times and downmodded
  <span class="negative_score">[% downs | html %]</span> times.
</p>
[% IF c.stash.person %]
<p>[% person(c.stash.thing) %] is also a person!</p> [% END %]
[% INCLUDE pair.tt2
  left_title = "Reasons why " _ c.stash.thing _ " is loved"
  right_title = "Reasons why " _ c.stash.thing _ " is hated"
  left = list_reasons(up_reasons)
  right = list_reasons(down_reasons)
  width = "50em"
%]
<div class="pair" style="width: 50em">
  <div class="box" style="padding-left: 13em; padding-right: 13em;">
    [% IF neutral_reasons.size > 0 %]
    <h3>Reasons why [% c.stash.thing | html %] is meh</h3> [%
      list_reasons(neutral_reasons) %]
    [% END %]
  </div>
</div>
```

We include our usual macros and then define one to format the up/down/neutral reasons into HTML. Then we start the actual body of the page, which is a bit of text showing the upmod and downmod count, and then a pair of reason lists. If we find a person that has the same name as thing, we display a link to that page. Below the pair of reason lists, we display the neutral reasons if there are any.

The final thing we need to do is to give each person a page, so that the `person()` links we create everywhere actually work. This page will show a list of the user's favorite and least favorite things and a list of machines that he has used.

We can create the Controller for `People` by the following command:

```
perl script/chatstat_create.pl controller People
```

Change the index Controller method to the following:

```
sub one_person :Path :Args(1) {
  my ($self, $c, $name) = @_;
  $c->stash(template => 'person.tt2');
  # find who we're looking for
  my $person  = $c->model('DBIC::People')->find($name, {key =>
    'nickname'});
  $c->stash->{person} = $person;
  $c->detach('/error_404', [qq{No such person "$name"}]) unless
    $person;
  # get nicknames
  my $nicknames = $person->nicknames;
  $c->stash->{nicknames} = $nicknames;
  my $nickids = [$nicknames->get_column('nid')->all];
  my @cond = ( { 'opinions.nid' =>
                  { -in => $nickids },
                },
                { join => 'opinions' }
            );
  # and do the search for things' scores
  my $t = $c->model('DBIC::Things');
  my @high  = $t->highest_rated->search(@cond);
  $c->stash->{high} = [@high];
  my @low   = $t->lowest_rated->search(@cond);
  $c->stash->{low} = [@low];
}
```

We start by finding the requested person, and detaching to a 404 page if it doesn't exist. The code for the 404 page is in `Root.pm`:

```
sub error_404 :Private {
  my ($self, $c, $reason) = @_;
  $reason ||= 'Not found';
  $c->stash(reason => $reason);
  $c->stash(template => '404.tt2');
  $c->response->status(404);
}
```

And the template, `root/src/404.tt2`:

```
<h2>404 Not Found</h2>
<p>[% reason | html %]</p>
<a href="[% c.uri_for('/') %]">Go home</a>? [% END %]
```

After we have a `Person`, we get a list of the nickname IDs that he/she has used, and use that data to build up some constraints that will limit a query of opinions to ones by that user. Finally, we use our `highest_rated` and `lowest_rated` resultsets methods to get the highest and lowest rated items, but with a twist—we search within that ResultSet and limit it to the nicknames used by the requested `Person`. In this way, we get a top and bottom ten list for a specific user.

Once we have the data, we just need to show it via `root/src/person.tt2`:

```
[% PROCESS thing_macros.tt2 %] [% INCLUDE pair.tt2
  title= c.stash.person.name _ "'s Notables" left_title = 'Ten
    Favorite Things'
  left = list_things(high)
  right_title = 'Ten Favorite Things to Hate' right =
    list_things(low)
%]
<h2>Known aliases</h2>
<table>
  <tr><th>user</th><th>nick</th><th>host</th></tr> [% WHILE (nick =
    nicknames.next) %]
  <tr>
    <td>[% nick.username | html %]</td>
    <td>[% person(nick.nick)  %]</td>
    <td>[% nick.host  | html %]</td>
  </tr>
[% END %]
</table>
```

Here, we reuse the `list_things` macro we wrote for the main page and show the pair of best/worst things. Then we use the `Person` object to display some information about the nicknames that person has used.

For completeness, let's also add an action for displaying a list of all people to the `People` Controller, `lib/ChatStat/Controller/People.pm`:

```
sub everyone :Path Args(0) {
  my ($self, $c) = @_;
  my $people = $c->model('DBIC::People');
  $c->stash->{people} = $people;
  $c->stash(template => 'people.tt2');
}
```

The template is simple (`root/src/people.tt2`):

```
[% PROCESS thing_macros.tt2 %]
<h2>Everyone</h2>
<ul>
  [% WHILE (the_person = people.next) %]
  <li>[% person(the_person.name) %]</li> [% END %]
</ul>
[% END %]
```

That's all we need for the read-only part of the interface. Everything that's linked to it works.

Let us add one last feature to the `Things` Controller to demonstrate Catalyst's chained dispatch type. We'll provide two additional actions, "ups" and "downs" to get just a list of up reasons and down reasons for each thing. The URL will look like `/things/<the thing>/ups` and `/things/<the thing>/downs`.

Without the chained dispatch type, writing something like this would be ugly. You would have to get the second argument (if there was one), figure out whether it was up or down, and then do something based on that information. Chained makes this sort of thing trivial.

To get started, we'll modify the existing actions a bit. Instead of:

```
sub one_thing :Path Args(1) {
  my ($self, $c, $thing) = @_;
  my $o = $c->model('DBIC::Opinions');
  my $m = $c->model('DBIC');
  # Aggregates
  $c->stash(template => "thing.tt2");
  $c->stash(thing  => $thing);
```

```
    $c->stash(points => $o->karma_for($thing));
    $c->stash(ups   => $o->karma_for($thing, 1));
    $c->stash(downs   => $o->karma_for($thing, -1));
    $c->stash(person  => $m->resultset('People')->find({ name =>
      $thing}, { key => 'nickname' })
    );
    # detailed reasons
    my @reasons = $c->model('DBIC::Things')->reasons_for($thing);
    my @up_r = grep { $_->points >  0 } @reasons; my @dn_r = grep {
      $_->points <  0 } @reasons; my @nu_r = grep { $_->points == 0 }
    @reasons;
    $c->stash(up_reasons  => \@up_r);
    $c->stash(down_reasons  => \@dn_r);
    $c->stash(neutral_reasons => \@nu_r);
  }
```

We'll start a chain as follows:

```
  sub thing_setup :Chained('/') PathPart('things') CaptureArgs(1) {
    my ($self, $c, $thing) = @_;
    $c->stash(thing => $thing);
    my $o = $c->model('DBIC::Opinions');
    my $m = $c->model('DBIC');
    # rest of the action, except setting the template
    $c->stash(thing => $thing);
    $c->stash(points => $o->karma_for($thing));
    $c->stash(ups => $o->karma_for($thing, 1));
    $c->stash(downs => $o->karma_for($thing, -1));
    $c->stash(person => $m->resultset('People')->find({ name =>
      $thing}, { key => 'nickname' })
    );
    # detailed reasons
    my @reasons = $c->model('DBIC::Things')->reasons_for($thing);
    my @up_r = grep { $_->points >  0 } @reasons; my @dn_r = grep {
      $_->points <  0 } @reasons; my @nu_r = grep { $_->points == 0 }
    @reasons;
    $c->stash(up_reasons  => \@up_r);
    $c->stash(down_reasons  => \@dn_r);
    $c->stash(neutral_reasons => \@nu_r);
  }
```

This code will start a chain. The chain is started when the URL request is of the form /things. This is derived from the following line:

```
sub thing_setup :Chained('/') PathPart('things') CaptureArgs(1) {
```

where we mention that the chain starts with / and the path in the URL is things. So it is /things.

Every chained Controller can have multiple methods as part of the chain. The last method in the chain is called the end point. From our last example, where we want to do things/up and things/down, we can handle this with two methods in the chain: /things as the start of the chain and up or down as the last method in the chain. The last method in the chain is called an end point. Notice also how a chained Controller which is not an end point like the one above uses CaptureArgs instead of Args. CaptureArgs tells Catalyst how many arguments the chained Controller is expecting in the URL.

We will create two end points for up and down as follows:

```
sub ups :Chained('thing_setup') Args(0) {
  my ($self, $c) = @_;
  $c->stash(template => 'reasons_simple.tt2');
  $c->stash(things => $c->stash->{up_reasons});
}
sub downs :Chained('thing_setup') Args(0) {
  my ($self, $c) = @_;
  $c->stash(template => 'reasons_simple.tt2');
  $c->stash(things => $c->stash->{down_reasons});
}
```

In this case, we can omit PathPart, because it defaults to the name of the action (/ups or /downs), and that's what we want this time.

We can also set up an action to be executed when /things is called without /up or /down:

```
sub one_thing :Chained('thing_setup') PathPart('') Args(0) {
  my ($self, $c) = @_;
  $c->stash(template => 'thing.tt2');
}
```

Here we're chaining this endpoint of `thing_setup` with an empty name, and accepting no arguments. Note that in the middle of the chain you say `CaptureArgs`, but at an endpoint you just say `Args` as usual.

That's all we need to do to add actions that show only ups or downs on the page. The setup work happens in `thing_setup`, and the endpoints that chain off that do the minimum amount of work needed to show the page.

To see this in action, just create the template, `root/src/reasons_simple.tt2`:

```
Reasons for [% thing | html %]
<ul>
  [% FOREACH thing = things %]
  <li>[% thing.reason | html %]</li> [% END %]
</ul>
```

Adding a `/ups` or `/downs` off any thing's page's URL will now show the simple list of reasons for that `thing`.

> Note that you can chain chains from chains, so that you aren't limited to a URL like `/base/<argument>/endpoint`. You can chain as many times as you like, so `/base/ <argument>/something/<argument>/ endpoint` is perfectly legal (and useful).

Summary

In this chapter, we learned how to leverage Catalyst and `DBIx::Class` to perform complex database actions. We also explored how to write custom resultsets. We learned how to use a shell-like environment (REPL) for quick debugging of the application. We explored chained actions. We learned all this by building a Chat Stat application that used all of the above concepts. In the process, we also discovered the benefits of good practices such as placing the data logic into the model.

6
Building Your Own Model

In the last few chapters, we've seen how `DBIx::Class` can provide a powerful interface to your data. However, sometimes `DBIx::Class` is not the right tool for the job. Often situations may arise in which your application won't be able to access database tables directly and instead you'll need to access data through predefined stored procedures. In this case, `DBIx::Class` would be useless as you aren't able to read and modify objects with the usual SELECT, INSERT, UPDATE, and DELETE command set—everything must be done by calling a procedure and reading back the result.

In other cases, your data won't be in a database at all. Instead, you might choose to store and retrieve information from files in a directory.

In this chapter, we'll cover three common cases—mixing a procedural interface with a relational `DBIx::Class` interface, writing a database interface without `DBIx::Class`, and building a custom Model that doesn't use a database at all. The number of extensions for DBIC (`DBIx::Class`), and even its own functionality is still growing. However, it is always a good idea to check CPAN before writing your own model.

Creating a database model from scratch

In some cases, you'll have no use of any of DBIC's functionality. DBIC might not work with your database, or perhaps you're migrating a legacy application that has well-tested database queries, which you don't want to rewrite. In this sort of situation, you can write the entire database model manually.

In the next example, we'll use `Catalyst::Model::DBI` to set up the basic DBI layer and the write methods (like we did) to access the data in the model. As we have the AddressBook application working, we'll add a DBI model and write some queries against the AddressBook database.

First, we need to create the model. We'll call it `AddressDBI`:

```
$ perl script/addressbook_create.pl model AddressDBI DBI DBI:SQLite:
database
```

When you open the generated `AddressBook::Model::AddressDBI` file, you should see something like this:

```
package AddressBook::Model::AddressDBI;
use strict;
use base 'Catalyst::Model::DBI';
PACKAGE  ->config(
    dsn      => 'DBI:SQLite:database',
    user     => '',
    password => '',
    options  => {},
);
1; # magic true value required
```

Once you have this file, you can start adding methods. The database handle will be available via `$self->dbh`, and the rest is up to you. Let's add a `count_users` function as follows:

```
sub count_users {
  my $self = shift;
  my $dbh = $self->dbh;
  my $rows = $dbh->
  selectall_arrayref('SELECT COUNT(id) FROM user');
  return $rows->[0]->[0]; # first row, then the first column
}
```

Let's also add a `Test` Controller so that we can see if this method works. Firstly, create the `Test` Controller by running the following command:

```
$ perl script/addressbook_create.pl controller Test
```

Then add a quick test action as follows:

```
sub count_users : Local {
  my ($self, $c) = @_;
  my $count = $c->model('AddressDBI')->count_users();
  $c->response->body("There are $count users.");
}
```

You can quickly see the output of this action by running the following command:

```
$ perl script/addressbook_test.pl /test/count_users
There are 2 users.
```

The `myapp_test.pl` script will work for any action, but it works best for such test actions because the output is plain text and will fit on the screen. When you're testing actual actions in your application, it's usually easier to read the page when you view it in the browser. If you need to protect sensitive information, you can check `$c->debug` to see if you are in debug mode, and only provide the information in that case.

That's all there is to it—just add methods to `AddressDBI` until you have everything you need.

The only other thing you might want to do is to add the database configuration to your `config` file, like we did in *Chapter 4, Expanding the Application*. It works almost the same way for DBI as it does for `DBIC::Schema`:

```
---
name: AddressBook
Model::AddressDBI:
dsn: "DBI:SQLite:database" username: ~
password: ~
options:
option1: something
# and so on
# the rest of your config file goes here
```

Extending a DBIx::Class model

A common occurrence is a situation in which your application has free reign over most of the database, but needs to use a few stored procedure calls to get to certain pieces of data. In that case, you'll want to create a normal DBIC schema, and then add methods for accessing the unusual data.

As an example, let's look back at the AddressBook application and imagine that for some reason we couldn't use `DBIx::Class` to access the `user` table, and instead need to write the raw SQL to return an array containing everyone's username. In `AddressBook::Model::AddressDB`, we just need to write a subroutine to do our work as follows:

```
package AddressBook::Model::AddressDB;
// other code in the package
sub get_users {
  my $self = shift;
  my $storage = $self->storage;
```

```
  return $storage->dbh_do(
    sub {
      my $self  = shift;
      my $dbh   = shift;
      my $sth   = $dbh->prepare('SELECT username FROM user');
      $sth->execute();
      my @rows = @{$sth->fetchall_arrayref()};
      return map { $_->[0] } @rows;
    });
}
```

Here's how the code works. On the first line, we get our `DBIC::Schema` object and then obtain the schema's `storage` object. The `storage` object is what DBIC uses to execute its generated SQL on the database, and is usually an instance of `DBIx::Class::Storage::DBI`. This class contains a method called `dbh_do` that will execute a piece of code, passed to `dbh_do` as a coderef (or "anonymous subroutine"), and provide the code with a standard DBI database handle (usually called `$dbh`). `dbh_do` will make sure that the database handle is valid before it calls your code, so you don't need to worry about things like the database connection timing out. DBIC will reconnect if necessary and will then call your code. `dbh_do` will also handle exceptions raised within your code in a standard way, so that errors can be caught normally.

The rest of the code deals with actually executing our query. When the database handle is ready, it's passed as the second argument to our coderef (the first is the `storage` object itself, in case you happen to need that). Once we have the database handle, the rest of the code is exactly the same as if we were using plain DBI instead of `DBIx::Class`. We first prepare our query (which need not be a `SELECT`; it could be `EXEC` or anything else), execute it and, finally, process the result. The `map` statement converts the returned data to the form we expect it in, a list of names (instead of a list of rows each containing a single name). Note that the `return` statement in the coderef returns to `dbh_do`, not to the caller of `get_users`. This means that you can execute `dbh_do` as many times as required and then further process the results before returning from the `get_users` subroutine.

Once you've written this subroutine, you can easily call it from elsewhere in your application as follows:

```
my @users = $c->model('AddressDB')->get_users;
$c->response->body('All Users' join ', ', @users);
```

Custom methods without raw SQL

As the last example doesn't use any features of the database that DBIC doesn't explicitly expose in its resultset interface, let us see how we can implement the get_users function without using dbh_do. Although the preconditions of the example indicated that we couldn't use DBIC, it's good to compare the two approaches so that you can decide which way to do things in your application. Here's another way to implement the last example:

```
sub get_users {
  # version 2
  my $self = shift;
  my $users = $self->resultset('User');
  my @result;
  while(my $user = $users->next){
    push @result, $user->username;
  }
  return @result;
}
```

This looks like the usual DBIC manipulation that we're used to. Usually, we call `$c->model('AddressDB::User')` to get the User resultset, but under the hood this is the same as `$c->model('AddressDB')->resultset('User')`. In this example, `$self` is the same as `$c->model('AddressDB')`.

The last code snippet is cleaner and more portable (across database systems) than the dbh_do method, so it's best to prefer resultsets over dbh_do unless there's absolutely no other way to achieve the functionality you desire.

Calling database functions

Another common problem is the need to call database functions on tables that you're accessing with DBIC. Fortunately, DBIC provides syntax for this case, so we won't need to write any SQL manually and run it with dbh_do. All that's required is a second argument to search. For example, if we want to get the count of all users in the user table, we could write (in a Controller) the following:

```
$users = $c->model('AddressDB::User');
$users->search({}, { select => [ { COUNT => 'id' } ],
as => [ 'count' ],});
$count = $users->first->get_column('count');
```

This is the same as executing SELECT COUNT(id) FROM user, fetching the first row, and then setting $count to the first column of that row.

 Note that we didn't specify a WHERE clause, but if we wanted to, we could replace the first { } with the WHERE expression, and then get the count of matching rows.

Here's a function that we can place in the User ResultSet class to get easy access to the user count:

```
sub count_users_where {
  my $self = shift;
  my $condition = shift;
  $self->search($condition,
  { select => [ { COUNT => 'id' } ], as => [ 'count' ], });
  my $first = $users->first;
  return $first->get_column('count') if $first;
  return 0; # if there is no "first" row, return 0
}
```

Now, we can write something like the following:

```
$jons = $c->model('AddressDB::User')->
count_users_where([ username => {-like => '%jon%'}]);
```

to get the number of jons in the database, without having to fetch every record and count them.

If you need to work only with a single column, you can also use the DBIx::Class::ResultSetColumn interface.

Implementing a Filesystem model

In this final example, we'll build an entire model from scratch without even the help of a model base class like Catalyst::Model::DBI. Before you do this for your own application, you should check the CPAN to see if anyone's done anything similar already. There are currently about fifty ready-to-use model base classes that abstract data sources, such as LDAP servers, RSS readers, shopping carts, search engines, subversion, e-mail folders, web services, and even YouTube. Expanding upon one of these classes will usually be easier than writing everything yourself.

For this example, we'll create a very simple blog application. To post the blog, you just write some text and put it in a file whose name is the title you want on the post. We'll write a Filesystem model from scratch to provide the application with the blog posts.

Let's start by creating the application's skeleton:

```
$ catalyst.pl Blog
```

After that, we'll create our Filesystem model:

```
$ cd Blog
$ perl script/blog_create.pl model Filesystem
```

We'll also use plain TT for the View:

```
$ perl script/blog_create.pl view TT TT
```

Let's continue by creating a template for displaying the most recent blog posts called root/recent.tt:

```
<html>
<head><title>Recent blog posts</title></head>
<body>
  <h1>Blog</h1>
  [% FOREACH post = posts %]
  <h2>[% post.title | html %]</h2>
  <i>Written on [% post.created | html %]</i> [% post.body %]
  [% END %]
  </body>
</html>
```

Finally, let's replace the default index action with one that gets the posts from the model and then displays them inside the recent.tt template. In Blog::Controller::Root, we'll replace default with the following code:

```
sub default : Path Args {
  my ( $self, $c ) = @_;
  $c->stash->{template} = 'recent.tt';
  #$c->stash->{posts} = [$c->model('Filesystem')
  #  ->get_recent_posts()];
}
```

Note that we've commented out the line where we get the posts; as we haven't implemented the get_recent_posts method yet, you should be able to start the application now and see the beginnings of a blog when you visit http://localhost:3000/.

All that's left to do is implement the model. This model will take a two-tiered approach. The actual Catalyst model will find all "posts" and will create a `Blog::Model::Filesystem::Post` object for each. These objects will do most of the work such as reading the file and so on. Let's start by creating the `Post` class by writing `lib/Blog/Model/Filesystem/Post.pm`:

```perl
# Post.pm
package Blog::Model::Filesystem::Post;
use strict; use warnings; use Carp;
use File::Basename;
use File::Slurp qw(read_file);
use File::CreationTime qw(creation_time);
use base 'Class::Accessor';
  PACKAGE  ->mk_ro_accessors(qw(filename));
sub new {
  my $class  = shift;
  my $filename = shift;
  croak "Must specify a filename" unless $filename;
  my $self = {};
  $self->{filename} = $filename;
  bless $self, $class;
  return $self;
}
sub title {
  my $self  = shift;
  my $filename = $self->filename;
  my $title  = basename($filename);
  $title  =~ s/[.](\w+)$//; # strip off .extensions return $title;
}
sub body {
  my $self = shift;
  return read_file($self->filename);
}
sub created {
  my $self = shift;
  return creation_time($self->filename);
}
sub modified {
  my $self = shift;
  return (stat $self->filename)[9]; # 9 is mtime
}
1;
```

This is a pretty standard Perl class. The new method takes a filename and creates an instance of this class based on the filename. The rest of the methods access the file and return the desired information. Because of the way we've designed the class, it will be extremely simple to add more information to each blog post in the future. We'll just create another method, and the information will be easily available to the Controller and the template.

Now we need to create the actual Catalyst model that will find blog posts and return instances of the `Post` object. To start with, we'll just need to add the `get_recent_posts` method in the following manner:

```
package Blog::Model::Filesystem;
use strict;
use warnings;
use base 'Catalyst::Model';
use Carp;
use File::Spec;
use Blog::Model::Filesystem::Post;
  PACKAGE  ->mk_accessors('base');
sub get_recent_posts {
  my $self = shift;
  my $base = $self->base;
  my @articles;
  opendir my $dir, $base or
  croak "Problem opening $base: $!";
  while(my $file = readdir $dir){
    next if $file =~ /^[.]/; # skip hidden files
    my $filename = File::Spec->catfile($base, $file);
    next if -d $filename;
    push @articles,
    Blog::Model::Filesystem::Post->new($filename);
  }
  closedir $dir;
  @articles = reverse sort {$a->created <=> $b->created}
  @articles;
  return @articles if @articles < 5;
  return @articles[0..4]; # top 5 otherwise
}
```

The `mk_accessors` line is especially important—this will allow you to specify a `base` attribute in the `config` file, which will then be available in the rest of the methods as `$self->base`. Here's the `config` file, `blog.yml`:

```
---
name: Blog
Model::Filesystem:
base: /tmp/test
```

Now all you need to do is remove the comment from the line in `Root.pm` and then add some HTML files to `/tmp/test`. When you start your server, you should see the five most recent posts displayed!

If you're interested in taking this idea further, check out the Angerwhale blogging system, available from the CPAN. It uses a similar filesystem-based model, but one that has many more features.

As Catalyst is now based on Moose, it might be a good idea to implement models using it. There are already specialized Moose roles for components on CPAN. In the next chapter, you will learn more about Moose and its application.

Tweaking the model

With the core functionality in place, we can now dig a bit deeper into the model and add some more features. The first one is a sort of "user interface" improvement. Instead of making the user type out the `Model::Filesystem` part in the `config` file, it would be nice to just specify `base` and have that take the effect in the same way. We can achieve this by reading the value of `$c->config->{base}` into `$c->config->{Model::Filesystem}->{base}` just before Catalyst creates an instance of the class. This is done by overriding the `COMPONENT` method in the model.

The `COMPONENT` method is called to set up things such as configuration, right before the new method is called (things like database connections are set up). We can override this in our model, tweak the config, and then call the version of `COMPONENT` in `Catalyst::Model` to finish up everything:

```
sub COMPONENT {
  my ($class, $app, $args) = @_;
  $args->{base} = $app->config->{base};
  return $class->NEXT::COMPONENT($app, $args);
}
```

With this code in place, we can change the `config` file to:

```
---
base: /tmp/test name: Blog
```

The last feature we'll add is validation of `base` in the new method. This will check to see if the base directory exists and if it does not, issue an error message and prevent the application from starting:

```
sub new {
  my $class = shift;
  my  $self = $class->NEXT::new(@_); # get the real self my  $base =
    $self->base;
  croak "base $base does not exist" if !-d $base;
  return $self;
}
```

If you're inheriting from a base class, you can control whether or not your code runs before that of your base class, by choosing whether to run your code before or after the `NEXT::new()` call. `NEXT::new()` is where the superclasses get a chance to set up themselves, and then control is passed back to you. You should return the result of `NEXT::new()` from the new method.

Request context inside the model

Generally, your model's configuration won't change as requests run. When Catalyst is started, your model is initialized and it doesn't see the rest of your application again. This means that you can't save the `$app` you got from COMPONENT and use it to, say, access `$c->request` or `$c->response` in the future. It's generally a good idea to avoid touching the request from inside a model anyway (that's what the Controller is for) , but if you absolutely need to, you can get the latest `$c` by implementing an ACCEPT_CONTEXT method in your model. It's called by Catalyst every time you call `$c->model()` and is passed `$c`, and any arguments are passed to `$c->model()`. In general, it will look something like this:

```
__PACKAGE__ ->mk_accessors(qw|context|); # at the top
sub ACCEPT_CONTEXT {
  my ($self, $c, @args) = @_;
  $self->context($c);
  return $self;
}
```

We return `$self` from ACCEPT_CONTEXT here, but in theory you can return anything. The value is passed directly back to the caller of `$c->model()`. DBIC::Schema takes advantage of this feature to return individual resultsets instead of the entire schema depending on how `$c->model()` is invoked.

After you've added an `ACCEPT_CONTEXT` method like we just did, you can call `$self->context()` anywhere in your model to get the current request context. There is now a component role on CPAN that can be implemented and does this readily and cleanly, and in a way that the user doesn't have to maintain for themselves in the future. You will learn more about this in the next chapter on Moose.

Maintainable models

When you're writing your own data model for use with Catalyst, you might want to consider making it work without Catalyst first, and then later adding some glue to make it easy to use from within Catalyst. The advantage of this approach is that you can test your model without having a Catalyst application to use it and that you can use your data model class in non-Catalyst applications, most commonly command-line scripts and background processes. `DBIx::Class` takes this approach; the `DBIx::Class::Schema` works fine without Catalyst. The DBIC model you create for your application is just a bit of glue to make using the `DBIx::Class::Schema` from Catalyst convenient.

Let's take a look at how we would build the Filesystem model in this manner. First, we'll move the `Blog::Model::Filesystem::Post` class to the `Blog::Backend::Filesystem::Post` namespace. Then, we'll write our post access code in `Blog::Backend::Filesystem` instead of `Blog::Model::Filesystem`. The code is exactly the same, except that we'll write our own new method as follows:

```
package Blog::Backend::Filesystem;
use strict; use warnings; use Carp;
use Blog::Backend::Filesystem::Post;
sub new {
  my ($class, $args) = @_; # args is { base => 'path' }
  croak 'need a base that exists' if !-d $args->{base};
  return bless $args, $class;
}
# then the same as Blog::Model::Filesystem above, substituting
# Blog::Model::Filesystem::Post for
# Blog::Backend::Filesystem::Post.
```

Now you have a class that you can use to access blog posts from outside of Catalyst. Just instantiate it like my `$post_model = Blog::Backend::Filesystem->new({ base => '/var/blog' })` and then use `$post_model` like you did `$c->model('Filesystem')`.

The final step is to create the glue to bind the backend class to a Catalyst model. Fortunately, `Catalyst::Model::Adaptor`, a module on CPAN, will do that for us automatically by running the following command:

```
$ perl script/blog_create.pl model Filesystem Adaptor Blog::Backend::
Filesystem
```

This command will create a model called `Blog::Model::Filesystem` that simply returns a `Blog::Backend::Filesystem` object when you call `$c->model('Filesystem')`. It works by creating a subclass of `Catalyst::Model::Adaptor` that will create an instance of your backend class at startup and return it when needed.

One disadvantage is that the configuration format changes slightly:

```
--- Model::Filesystem:
args:
base: /var/blog
```

If you want to avoid the unsightly `args` key, you can override `prepare_arguments` in the model like this:

```
package Blog::Model::Filesytem;
# generated code here sub prepare_arguments {
  my ($self, $app) = @_;
  return { base => $app->{base} };
}
```

Now the adapted Filesystem model will work exactly like the one we made earlier, but with very little Catalyst-specific code.

If you are writing a model that needs a new backend class created every time you call `$c->model` or once per request (instead of once per application), you can use the `Catalyst::Model::Factory` and `Catalyst::Model::Factory::PerRequest` modules included with `Catalyst::Model::Adaptor`. They are all used in the same way (as we just saw, substituting `Factory` or `Factory::PerRequest` for `Adaptor`), but integrate your backend class with Catalyst in slightly different ways. For most cases, these models will be all you need.

Other components

Models are just the tip of the iceberg—Views and Controllers work the same way (and implement the same methods) as Models. You can easily create custom Views and Controllers and inherit from them in your application to improve the reusability of your application's code.

Summary

In this chapter, we looked at alternate ways to access the data model. We first added the ability to execute raw SQL to a standard DBIC model, and contrasted the code with normal DBIC resultset access. Then, we completely eliminated DBIC and wrote a database Model that used DBI to run raw SQL on the database. Next, we created a Filesystem model from scratch, and learned how to use COMPONENT and ACCEPT_CONTEXT to integrate the Model with the Catalyst application. We also saw how using Catalyst::Model::Adaptor made writing a maintainable Model easier. Remember that the best practice is to always have the definition and behavior of the data in the model, which allows for the Controller to become a glue and as thin. The View can then be independent to render the data.

7
Hot Web Topics

Traditionally, web applications were lonely and isolated. Each of them had their own set of users and data, and never acknowledged the existence of other applications. Today, things are changing. Web applications provide public APIs so that other applications can programmatically interact with their data and users. Users can visit sites and later request that the site notifies them when it has been updated.

Another new development is the widespread adoption of dynamic JavaScript-enabled web applications. Gone are the days of slow waits between pages while things get loaded; AJAX allows web applications to be almost as responsive as native desktop applications. In this chapter, we'll take a look at how to get your Catalyst application in on the fun! We'll add a REST API to allow other programs to easily access our application. Then, we'll use this API to add AJAX interactivity to our application. Finally, we'll modify our mini-blog application to allow users to subscribe to the latest posts.

REST

A feature that many public websites are beginning to offer to their users is the ability to get the information out of the application through a well-defined **API** (**Application Programming Interface**). Instead of forcing users to "screen-scrape" the HTML (programmatically parsing the pages that normal browser-based visitors see on the screen), which is tedious and prone to error, the application provides developers with the ability to access the application's entities in a serialized (XML, JSON, and so on) format. Thanks to a wide variety of data deserializers for nearly every programming language, getting data from a web application into your application is extremely easy to implement and maintain with this approach.

There are two main methods of providing this functionality, **RPC (remote procedure call)**, such as XML-RPC or **SOAP (Simple Object Access Protocol)**, and **REST (Representational State Transfer)**. RPC-based approaches create an "RPC endpoint" URL for your application and clients send requests (like 'give me address 42' or 'delete person 10') to this URL and get responses back. All requests use the same endpoint.

REST uses a cleaner approach; it provides a URL for each entity ("noun") and the client uses HTTP verbs to operate on these. Instead of sending an HTTP GET request to /address/42/delete to delete address 42, we send an HTTP DELETE to /address/42. A GET request to that location would return the serialized address and a PUT request would update the data with the serialized version sent with the request. POST-ing to the /address URL will create a new address.

To understand REST, better think of a library project. In REST architecture, the URIs will be well formed and will follow a structure. For example, you will have the following URIs:

- Book/add
- Book/edit/1
- Book/delete/1
- Author/add

In addition to the URIs following a structure, you will also have to follow certain conventions, such as reading operations are always GET requests, a new entry is always a POST request, and so on.

In addition, all errors (and status indication) that can arise during this process are returned as standard HTTP codes. If an address isn't found, the REST interface returns '404 Not Found'. When an entity is created, the server returns '201 Created' along with the serialized entity. If a certain HTTP method doesn't make sense for a certain entity, '405 Method Not Allowed' is returned. There's no strict standard dictating what to return when, but the convention is to pick the most descriptive HTTP status code. The idea is to make it as easy as possible for an off-the-shelf HTTP client to understand what the response means.

For a more detailed reading on REST, After this line add the following two link:

http://tomayko.com/writings/rest-to-my-wife

http://en.wikipedia.org/wiki/Representational_State_Transfer

We'll see all of this in action as we add a REST interface to our AddressBook application.

Getting some REST

In this section, we'll add REST to the AddressBook application so that API clients can easily look up people and their addresses. We'll write a simple command-line client for accessing this interface, and we'll use it in the next section to implement an interactive JavaScript interface.

The first step is to install one of Catalyst's REST implementations, `Catalyst::Controller::REST` (found in the `Catalyst::Action::REST` distribution). `Catalyst::Controller::REST` is a Controller base class that will handle most of the REST details for us. It will automatically determine the type of incoming data and deserialize it into a Perl object. When we send a response, it will automatically serialize the response entity into the format that the client requested. It also adds some convenience functions, so we don't have to remember the proper HTTP response codes for each operation. Finally, it includes an ActionClass that will dispatch different HTTP methods to different Perl methods. We'll make use of all these features when creating the REST interface.

REST Controller

To provide a clean namespace for our REST actions, we're going to implement the REST interface in a separate controller called "REST". Let's start by creating `/lib/AddressBook/Controller/REST.pm` as follows:

```
package AddressBook::Controller::REST;
use strict;
use warnings;
use base qw(Catalyst::Controller::REST);
__PACKAGE__->config->{serialize}{default} = 'JSON';
1;
```

This creates the basic Controller, and sets the default serialization method to **JSON (JavaScript Object Notation)**. Clients can override this by sending a standard HTTP `Accept:` header. They specify the format that their `PUT` or `POST` request is in by setting a `Content-type:` header. Formats supported by `Catalyst::Controller::REST` include JSON, YAML, XML, raw PHP, raw Perl, FreezeThaw, and Storable. Refer to the following documentation for a full list and what headers to send for each type:

`http://search.cpan.org/~bobtfish/Catalyst-Action-REST-0.85/lib/Catalyst/Controller/REST.pm`

REST authentication

Before we write any more code, we need to think about how to handle authentication for the REST interface. As users of the API will most likely not be using a browser, requiring them to log in, get a cookie, and send it with each request would be cumbersome. As a result, REST (and RPC) interfaces usually use some other sort of authentication.

The most common method (used by Flickr and Google, among many others) is to give each user an **API key**. The API key works like a username and password, but can be disabled if the user abuses the API (without disabling his normal web access). The API key is sent in the headers of every request and the REST interface verifies it before performing the request.

As it seems unlikely that anyone would abuse our AddressBook's API, we'll just send the normal username and password with every request. As there's no standard HTTP header for this, we'll use X-Username and X-Password.

In addition, we'll want the REST interface to work (partially) from a web browser. So, we will also check to see if a user is logged in through the normal cookie method. If he/she is, we won't bother checking for the X-Username and X-Password headers.

Every REST request will need to be authenticated, so we'll add the authentication check in the begin method of the REST Controller as follows:

```
sub begin : ActionClass('Deserialize') {
  my ($self, $c) = @_;
  my $username = $c->req->header('X-Username');
  my $password = $c->req->header('X-Password');
  # require either logged in user, or correct user+pass in headers
  if ( !$c->user && !$c->login($username, $password) ){
    # login failed
    $c->res->status(403); # forbidden
    $c->res->body("You are not authorized to use the REST API.");
    $c->detach;
  }
}
```

Note that we are also applying the Deserialize action class here. Normally, the REST Controller deserializes the request automatically, but we're overriding it's begin method where it would perform this task. So, we re-add it explicitly so that everything continues to work normally.

We also need to tell our normal ACL plugin to ignore the REST area, so at the bottom of AddressBook.pm, we add the following line:

```
__Package__->allow_access('/rest'); # rest does its own auth
```

Adding an entity

Now that our interface is protected appropriately, we can start adding some entities. The format for implementing REST entities with Catalyst::Controller::REST is as follows. We first create a standard Catalyst action that acts as the entity (noun). We use the normal :Local, :Global, :Path, and other attributes to map the action to a URL. However, we also add the REST action class to the action. This action class will eliminate some tedium associated with REST. Instead of a chain of if statements like the following:

```
if ($c->req->method eq 'GET') { handle GET request }
elsif($c->req->method eq 'POST'){ handle POST request }
elsif( ... ) ...
else { return an error }
```

we can write the following:

```
sub entity :Local :ActionClass('REST'){
  # do some setup for each request
}
sub entity_GET  { handle GET request }
sub entity_POST { handle POST request }
```

Catalyst will take care of returning an HTTP error code when a method isn't implemented, and will also allow an HTTP client to ask what methods are implemented for a given entity.

Let us apply this by creating the shell of a person entity as follows:

```
sub person :Local :ActionClass('REST') Args(1) {
  my ($self, $c, $id) = @_;
  $c->stash(id => $id);
}
sub person_GET {
  my ($self, $c) = @_;
  my $id = $c->stash->{id};
  my $person = $c->model('AddressDB::People')->
  find({id => $id});
  if ($person) {
    $self->status_ok($c, entity =>
    mk_person_entity($person));
  }
  else {
    $self->status_not_found($c, message =>
    'No matching person found');
  }
}
```

```perl
sub mk_person_entity {
  my $person = shift;
  my $addresses =
  [ map {
      mk_address_entity($_)->{address}
    }
    $person->addresses
  ];
  return { person => { firstname => $person->firstname,
    lastname        => $person->lastname,
    fullname        => $person->name,
    id              => $person->id,
    addresses       => $addresses,
    }
  };
}
```

Here, we create the main person action, which optionally accepts an ID number and implements the GET method. Notice that we use some convenience methods in `Catalyst::Controller::REST` to handle the HTTP plumbing for us. When a record is found successfully, we call `status_ok` with the entity. When a record is not found, we call `status_not_found` with an error message. These two methods will send the appropriate HTTP response codes (200 and 404, respectively) and will serialize the provided entity and error message with the client's serializer of choice.

One thing to watch out for is that we don't implement the `mk_address_entity` method until later in the chapter. So for testing purposes, comment out the `map {}` statement and the `address => $addresses` hash entry for now.

Once you've added this code, you're ready to test your first REST action! Start the development server, open a web browser, and point it to `http://localhost:3000/rest/person/1`. Depending on what headers your browser sends, you'll either see an XML version of the `person` object:

```xml
<opt>
  <data id="1" name="person" firstname="Jonathan"
  fullname="Jonathan Rockway" lastname="Rockway" />
</opt>
```

or perhaps a YAML version:

```yaml
---
person:
firstname: Jonathan
fullname: Jonathan Rockway
id: 1
lastname: Rockway
```

And if your browser sends no `Accept` header at all, you'll see the JSON fallback:

```
{"person":{"firstname":"Jonathan","lastname":"Rockway","id":1,
  "fulname:"Jonathan Rockway"}}
```

As you can see, regardless of the format returned, the information is much easier to reuse than it would be without the API.

Now that we have the basic idea of REST, let's add a PUT method for updating the existing records:

```
sub person_PUT {
  my ($self, $c) = @_;
  my $id = $c->stash->{id};
  my $person = $c->model('AddressDB::People')->
  find_or_new({id => $id});
  if ($person) {
    $person->firstname ($c->req->data->{firstname})
    if $c->req->data->{firstname};
    $person->lastname  ($c->req->data->{lastname} )
    if $c->req->data->{lastname};
    $person->insert_or_update;
    $self->status_created($c,
      entity =>
        mk_person_entity($person),
      location =>
        $c->
         uri_for("/rest/person/$id"));
  }
  else {
    $self->status_not_found($c,
    message => 'No matching person found');
  }
}
```

This looks similar to GET, but we actually update the record with data from the serialized request (available via `$c->req->data`). When we update the record successfully, we return a '201 Created' response. By convention, we include the URL where this object can be requested, but we also include the object so that the client doesn't have to make another request. REST is flexible; you can use both a location and an entity, or just one of them.

We're not doing any data validation here (other than not changing fields that aren't sent). In a real application, you'll want to factor the validation code out of the `Person` Controller (and into the model, usually) and share it between the REST and non-REST interface. When the data is invalid, simply return a '400 Bad Request', which tells the client to not repeat the request without changing the data.

With PUT done, we need a way to create a new record (without providing an ID).

POST serves the following purpose:

```
sub person_POST {
  my ($self, $c) = @_;
  my $person = $c->model('AddressDB::People')->
  create({ firstname => $c->req->data->{firstname},
    lastname => $c->req->data->{lastname},
  });
  my $id = $person->id;
  $self->status_created($c,
    entity =>
      mk_person_entity($person),
    location =>
      $c->uri_for("/rest/person/$id"));
}
```

Finally, we need a way to delete records:

```
sub person_DELETE {
  my ($self, $c) = @_;
  my $id = $c->stash->{id};
  my $person = $c->model('AddressDB::People')->
  find({id => $id});
  if ($person) {
    $self->status_ok($c,
      entity => mk_person_entity($person));
    $person->delete;
  }
  else {
    $self->status_not_found($c,
    message => 'No matching person found');
  }
}
```

In this example, we return a copy of the deleted object, but this isn't always necessary. It's perfectly fine for the DELETE method to delete the object and just return '200 OK'.

With the person entity out of the way, let us add an interface to the address objects. The procedure is exactly the same:

```
sub address : Local : ActionClass('REST'){
  my ($self, $c, $id) = @_;
  $c->stash(id => $id);
}
sub address_GET {
  my ($self, $c) = @_;
  my $id = $c->stash->{id};
  my $address = $c->model('AddressDB::Addresses')->find({id =>
    $id});
  if ($address) {
    $self->status_ok($c, entity => mk_address_entity($address));
  }
  else {
    $self->status_not_found($c, message => 'No matching address
      found');
  }
}
sub address_PUT {
  my ($self, $c) = @_;
  my $id = $c->stash->{id};
eval {
  my $address = $c->model('AddressDB::Addresses')->
  find_or_new({id => $id});
  $address->location($c->req->data->{location})
  if $c->req->data->{location};
  $address->postal ($c->req->data->{postal})
  if $c->req->data->{postal};
  $address->phone ($c->req->data->{phone})
  if $c->req->data->{phone};
  $address->email ($c->req->data->{email})
  if $c->req->data->{email};
  $address->person ($c->req->data->{person})
  if $c->req->data->{person};
  $address->insert_or_update;
  $id = $address->id;
  $self->status_created($c,
    entity => mk_address_entity($address),
    location => $c->uri_for("/rest/address/$id"));
```

```
    };
    if ($@) {
      $self->status_bad_request($c,
      message => "Invalid data supplied: $@");
    }
  }
sub address_POST {
  my ($self, $c) = @_;
  eval {
    my $address = $c->model('AddressDB::Addresses')->
    create({ location => $c->req->data->{location},
      postal => $c->req->data->{postal},
      phone  => $c->req->data->{phone},
      email  => $c->req->data->{email},
      person => $c->req->data->{person},
    });
    my $id = $address->id;
    $self->status_created($c,
      entity => mk_address_entity($address),
      location => $c->uri_for("/rest/address/$id"));
  };
  if ($@) {
    $self->status_bad_request($c,
    message => "Invalid data supplied: $@");
  }
}
sub address_DELETE {
  my ($self, $c) = @_;
  my $id = $c->stash->{id};
  my $address = $c->model('AddressDB::Addresses')->
    find({id =>$id});
  if ($address) {
    $self->status_ok($c, entity => mk_address_entity($address));
    $address->delete;
  }
  else {
    $self->status_not_found($c, message => 'No matching address
      found');
  }
}
sub mk_address_entity {
  my $address = shift;
  return { address  => { id => $address->id,
      person          => $address->person->id,
      person_name     => $address->person->name,
      email           => $address->email,
```

```
        phone           => $address->phone,
        postal          => $address->postal,
        location        => $address->location,
    }
  };
}
```

Now that you have the `mk_address_entity` function, you can return the address records for a person when the person is requested, that is, you can remove the comments from the earlier lines.

This time we're doing a bit of validation. As the database might throw an exception when a foreign key or NOT NULL constraint is violated, we wrap database writes in an `eval {}` block. If there's a database error, we return '400 Bad Request' and the error message from the database. You'll probably want to return a more detailed error message in a real application, as your users probably don't care about what database constraints you have.

REST easy

That's all there is to creating an API for your application—give each object a URL and allow HTTP verbs as actions to perform on that object.

In the next section, we'll use our own REST API to implement AJAX.

AJAX

AJAX is a technique for dynamically adding new data to a web page that's already loaded. It technically stands for **asynchronous JavaScript and XML**, but the original meaning has been diluted such that AJAX also refers to synchronous JavaScript and JSON, as well. Think of it as DHTML that can dynamically retrieve data from the server in the background.

As JavaScript has matured greatly over the last few years and browser support is generally solid, so there's no reason to shy away from its use. A little JavaScript can greatly improve the user experience for users that choose to enable it.

In this section, we'll improve the AddressBook user interface a bit by adding some AJAX. The end goal is to be able to edit addresses "in place". Instead of clicking "edit" and waiting for the address editing page to load, the text fields will turn into textboxes and the user can begin editing immediately. When he's done, clicking **Submit** will submit the address for validation and the process will proceed as usual.

Getting started

The bulk of AJAX is getting the data from the server to the client in JSON or XML form. However, handling the JSON data on the client side is where most of the effort is spent. There are several frameworks that do this and they all work fine with Catalyst. Some of the most popular are Dojo, jQuery, MooTools, and prototype. Prototype is popular (and even has a Catalyst plugin), but it's hard to integrate with other JavaScript, so it's best to avoid it for maintainability reasons. The other frameworks have more features and cause fewer undesirable side effects.

For our application, we're going to take a more Perl-based approach and use a framework called **jemplate**. Jemplate is basically Template Toolkit for JavaScript. You send your TT template to the client along with some JSON, and the client will render it and update the web page accordingly. I prefer this approach because I can reuse my TT templates and my REST interface. (Other frameworks require that you send HTML back, so you have to write completely new actions and templates to satisfy them.)

Jemplate

Jemplate is actually a two-part framework. Half of it is the TT to JavaScript compiler, which runs inside our application. The other half is the JavaScript that runs in the client's browser. To get the Catalyst part, simply install `Catalyst::View::Jemplate` from CPAN. Then, run the following command line:

```
$ perl script/addressbook_create.pl view Jemplate Jemplate
```

Next, create `root/jemplate` where the jemplates will live and edit the `INCLUDE_PATH` in `AddressBook::View::HTML` to look like the following:

```
__PACKAGE__->config({
  INCLUDE_PATH => [
    AddressBook->path_to( 'root', 'jemplate'),
    AddressBook->path_to( 'root', 'src' ),
    AddressBook->path_to( 'root', 'lib' ),
  ],
});
```

This will allow TT to access the jemplates.

Continuing, we need to create an action in the `Root` Controller that will compile all the jemplates in the `jemplate` directory and send the JavaScript to the browser. (This sounds inefficient, but compilation only happens once, and both the server and client will cache the compiled results.)

In `lib/AddressBook/Controller/Root.pm`, add the following:

```
=head2 jemplate
Return the jemplates.
=cut
sub jemplate : Global {
  my($self, $c) = @_;
  $c->forward('View::Jemplate');
}
```

This will make the jemplate JavaScript available at `/jemplate`.

Lastly, we need to add a `Cache` backend to the application so that we can cache the compiled jemplates. Install `Catalyst::Plugin::Cache::Store::FastMmap` from the CPAN and then add `Cache` and `Cache::Store::FastMmap` to the `use Catalyst` line where you load the other plugins. Also, add the following configuration somewhere before `PACKAGE ->setup`:

```
__PACKAGE__->config->{cache}{expires} = 43200;
__PACKAGE__->config->{cache}{backends}{jemplate}{store} = 'FastMmap';
__PACKAGE__->config->{'View::Jemplate'}{jemplate_dir} =
__PACKAGE__->path_to('root', 'jemplate');
__PACKAGE__->config->{'View::Jemplate'}{jemplate_ext} = '.tt2';
```

This sets up a jemplate cache, shared between all instances of your application, using the `FastMmap` backend. We also configure the Jemplate compiler to treat `*.tt2` in `root/jemplates` as jemplates to compile and send to the client.

The final step is to generate the Jemplate runtime JavaScript as follows:

```
$ jemplate --runtime > root/static/Jemplate.js
```

and include it on every page by editing `root/lib/site/html` and adding the following lines in the `<head>` section:

```
<script type="text/javascript"
  src="[% base %]static/Jemplate.js"></script>
<script type="text/javascript"
  src="[% base %]jemplate"></script>
```

We're also including the compiled Jemplates, even though we haven't written any as yet. You only need that one line of JavaScript to include all the jemplates in the `jemplate` directory.

Implementing AJAX

Now that we've set up the Jemplate framework, we can start writing jemplates.

The basic workflow goes like this:

1. Create an action that supplies JSON to the client.
2. Write a Template Toolkit template to turn the JSON into HTML.

The syntax for a jemplate is the same as a regular template. If your JSON action returns a structure like {hello:world}, then you can access hello with the [% hello %] syntax in the template. (Arrays and hashes work too; jemplate is similar to Template Toolkit.) After that, you need to call Jemplate's process function on the client side with the filename of the template to use, the URL where the JSON can be fetched from, and the ID of the HTML DOM element to be replaced with the rendered text.

We'll see this in action by implementing the in-place address editor described earlier. The first step is to create a jemplate that will render an address' JSON (or Catalyst stash entry) as either an editable form or as a view-only piece of text. We'll use the view-only part to initially populate the View via TT, and then show the editable form via AJAX when requested. The same TT template will run on both the server and the client, which is the real power of jemplate.

The template will be called edit_address.tt2 and will live in the root/jemplate directory:

```
[% IF error %]
  <p class="error">[% error %]</p>
[% END %]
[% IF view_only %]
  <b>[% address.location | html %]</b>
  <a href="[% Catalyst.uri_for("/address/edit/$address.id") %]"
    onclick="show_address_edit_form([% address.id | html %]);
    return false;">
    Edit</a>
  <a href="[% Catalyst.uri_for("/address/delete/$address.id") %]">
    Delete</a>
  <br />
  <div class="address" id="address_[% address.id | html %]">
    <address>[% address.postal | html | html_line_break %]</address>
    Phone: [% address.phone | html %]<br />
    Email: [% address.email | html %]<br />
  </div>
[% ELSE %]
```

```
<form name="edit_address" method="post"
  action="../address/edit/[% address.id %]">
  <input name="_" type="hidden" value="_" />
  <input id="_submitted_address_edit"
    name="_submitted_address_edit" type="hidden" value="1" />
  <table>
    <tr>
      <td>Location</td>
      <td><input name="location"
          type="text" value="[% address.location | html %]" /></td>
    </tr>
    <tr valign="top">
      <td>Mailing Address</td>
      <td><textarea cols="60" name="postal"
          rows="4">[% address.postal | html %]</textarea></td>
    </tr>
    <tr valign="top">
      <td>Phone Number</td>
      <td><input name="phone" type="text"
          value="[% address.phone | html %]" /></td>
    </tr>
    <tr valign="top">
      <td>E-Mail Address</td>
      <td><input name="email" type="text"
          value="[% address.email %]" /></td>
    </tr>
    <tr valign="top">
      <td align="center" colspan="2"><input name="_submit"
        type="submit" Hot Web Topics [ 148 ]
        value="Submit" /></td>
    </tr>
  </table>
</form>
[% END %]
```

The HTML inside the form is copied from the `FormBuilder` output; we're going to trick `FormBuilder` into thinking that this is just a regular `FormBuilder` form so that we don't have to reimplement validation, and so on. (If the AJAX-submitted form is invalid, the user will just get the regular `FormBuilder` address editor page.)

As this template is mostly duplicating the functionality in `root/src/address_fragment.tt2`, we'll edit that file to just include the jemplate as follows:

```
[% INCLUDE "edit_address.tt2" view_only = 1 %]
```

You should be able to start the server now and navigate to the list of people and addresses. It should look exactly the same as before, as we haven't really changed anything yet. We only moved the `address_fragment` code into the `edit_address` template. We haven't added any JavaScript interactivity yet; everything is static HTML rendered by TT on the server.

Now let's add the interactivity. The basic idea is to make the edit link for each address call the jemplate process function instead of navigating to another page. We'll leave the `href` attribute of the link intact, so that users without JavaScript will not be affected. The basic pattern for this is as given:

```
<a href="non-javascript" onclick="function(); return false">
```

The `return false` tells the browser to not follow the `href` after the JavaScript function runs.

Now all that's left is to write that `function()`. As we're going to have multiple addresses on the same page, the function should only operate on a specific ID. When run, it should request the address data from `/rest/address/id` and render the template into a `#address_id div`. The code that does that looks like this:

```
function show_address_edit_form(id) {
  Jemplate.process('edit_address.tt2',
  '[% Catalyst.uri_for("/rest/address/") %]'+id,
  '#address_'+id);
}
```

That function should be placed in `root/lib/site/html`, in the `<head>` section, surrounded by `<script type="text/javascript"></script>` tags.

When we were editing the `edit_address.tt2` jemplate earlier, we changed the link to run that JavaScript function (for the correct ID). That's all we needed to do; everything is in place for the in-place editor to work. Start the server, navigate to the list of addresses, and click edit. The text of the address should be replaced with an editable form! That's AJAX.

If it's not working for you, you might want to try installing Firefox and the Firebug extension. Firebug will show you all JavaScript errors and AJAX requests (requests and responses with complete headers) and will let you set JavaScript breakpoints.

If something's wrong with the JavaScript, Firebug should help you identify the problem very quickly.

If you have that part working, let's add one more feature—the ability to cancel editing. All this feature does is request the jemplate again, but with editing disabled.

First we need to modify the `edit_address` jemplate to have another `div` to install the read-only version. Before the following line:

```
<b>[% address.location | html %]
```

add a wrapper `div`:

```
<div id="outside_address_[% address.id | html %]">
```

Also be sure to close that `div` with a `</div>` tag, just before the `[% ELSE %]` directive. At the very bottom of the file (or where your designer prefers), add a simple link:

```
<a href="#" onclick="cancel_address_edit([% address.id | html %]);
  return false">
  [X] Cancel edit
</a>
```

This is the link that will appear in the edit mode to allow the user to cancel the edit. Now, let us implement the `cancel_address_edit` function, which goes in the same place as the `show_address_edit_form` function:

```
function cancel_address_edit(id){
  var data = Ajax.get('[%
  Catalyst.uri_for("/rest/address/") %]'
  +id); data = JSON.parse(data); data.view_only = 1;
  var elem = document.getElementById('outside_address_'+id);
  Jemplate.process('edit_address.tt2', data, elem);
}
```

Here we are getting the response and converting it to JSON with `JSON.parse`, after which we are taking the converted JSON and setting the key `view_only` as 1. Then, we let JSON render the template. To be sure that the new version of the jemplate is used, do `rm -rf /tmp/addressbook` and restart the server. You should now be able to cancel the edit operation by clicking the link. Using the same template on both the client and the server is a powerful concept, and should make it easy for you to quickly implement a JavaScript-based user interface.

We can see a rendered in-place edit form, with Firebug on the lower half of the screenshot showing the AJAX response:

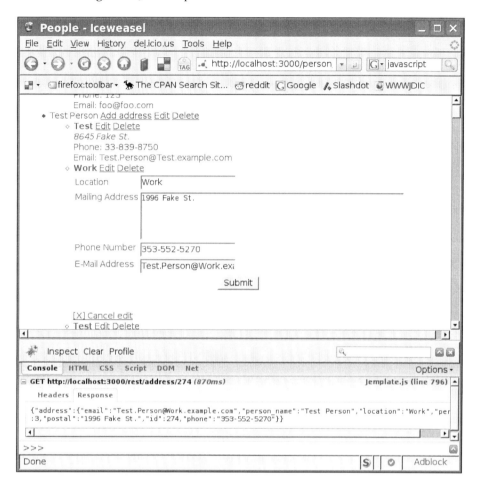

The cancelled in-place edit is seen in the following screenshot:

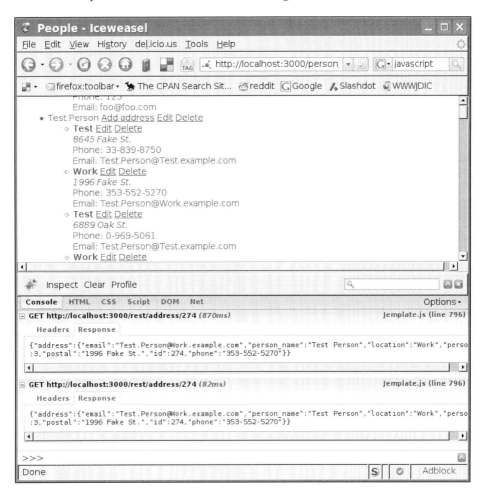

RSS

The final topic that we'll examine is RSS feeds. An RSS feed is an XML format designed to let users subscribe to a website and receive notification whenever a new article (or other piece of content) is posted. It works best for news sites or blogs.

RSS is beginning to be phased out in favor of Atom that serves the same purpose but is an actual IETF standard. Users use RSS and Atom interchangeably and most RSS readers support Atom feeds. We'll be using the XML::Feed CPAN module to generate the RSS feed, which can generate Atom and legacy RSS from the same code.

To demonstrate the concept of RSS, we'll add an RSS feed to our mini-blog program from *Chapter 6, Building Your Own Model*. To start, let's create a Controller to generate RSS feeds. As the RSS feed is specific to one piece of data and no templating system is used to generate the feed, we're going to do everything inside a Controller for demonstration. However, when building real application, always use a View.

Here's the source of the `Feeds` Controller:

```
(in Blog/lib/Blog/Controller/Feeds.pm):
package Blog::Controller::Feeds;
use strict;
use warnings;
use base 'Catalyst::Controller';
use XML::Feed;
use DateTime;
sub atom : Local {
  my ($self, $c) = @_;
  $c->stash->{type} = 'Atom';
}
sub rss : Local {
  my ($self, $c) = @_;
  $c->stash->{type} = 'RSS';
}
sub end : Private {
  my ($self, $c) = @_;
  my @posts = $c->model('Filesystem')->get_recent_posts;
  my $feed = XML::Feed->new($c->stash->{type});
  $feed->title("Test Blog Feed");
  $feed->link($c->uri_for('/'));
  $feed->description("Test feed for my mini-blog");
  $feed->author("Your Name");
  $feed->language('en-US');
  foreach my $post (@posts) {
    my $entry = XML::Feed::Entry->new($c->stash->{type});
    $entry->title($post->title);
    $entry->content($post->body);
    $entry->issued(DateTime->from_epoch(epoch => $post->created));
    $entry->modified(DateTime->from_epoch(epoch =>
      $post->modified));
    # entry unique ID
    $entry->link($c->req->base.$post->created.$post->title);
    $feed->add_entry($entry);
  }
  $c->res->content_type('application/xml');
  $c->res->body($feed->as_xml);
}
1;
```

Creating an RSS feed is very simple. The first two actions let the user select what type of feed he wants based on the URL. Regardless of choice, we forward to `end` action where we actually render the feed.

Here, we create an `XML::Feed` object and then set as many attributes as possible (the manual for `XML::Feed` shows the whole list of possible attributes). Then, for each blog post, we create an `XML::Feed::Entry`, populate it, and add it to the feed. At the very end, we send the generated XML to the user.

When a user subscribes to the feed, his client will request the feed every few hours. When a new article is added (as specified by "link", the article's unique ID), he'll be alerted that the site has changed. Most users prefer that the full text of the updated article be in the "content" field in the RSS entry (so that they can view the article right inside the RSS reader), but it's acceptable to only include the first paragraph so that the user will visit your site for the full story.

Summary

In this chapter, we developed a REST API to allow easy access to our application's data. We used this API to ease development of an interactive JavaScript interface to editing addresses. Finally, we added an RSS feed to our mini-blog to allow users to subscribe to the latest updates and posts.

8
Moose

Support for object orientation in Perl was added later on and one has to build these features into their packages from startup. However, fortunately, there are many packages that extend the object orientation of Perl, just like there are many templating engines. **Moose** is the most widely accepted and promising extension of Perl's object orientation. Catalyst itself as of version 5.8 is rewritten to use Moose. Moose is based on Class-MOP, which implements the **meta object protocol** (**MOP**) in Perl. This allows MooseX extensions to be used in combination in a single class without them bothering each other. It also makes classes inspectable, which allows for things such as form generation by reflection of class attributes. In this chapter, we will explore Moose and how Catalyst applications can benefit from it. This chapter assumes that you are already familiar with the basics of object-oriented programming in Perl.

Moose introduction

Moose introduces declarative syntax for objects in Perl similar to Ruby. Moose is just another package technically and it can be used like any other package by including it with `use Moose`.

OO in Perl

Following are some fundamentals of OO in Perl:

- **Every package is a class**: `package packagename` means that the code following in the rest of the scope is defining a class called `packagename`.

- **Every subroutine is a method**: Every subroutine in a class becomes an object method. Can be avoided by using `namespace::autoclean`.

- **An object is only a blessed reference**: Any reference that gets blessed is an object that can use the methods from the blessing class.

We are familiar with the following in the context of a class:

- Properties
- Methods that can manipulate these properties
- Ways of instantiating itself as objects

Let us explore how Perl addresses this. Properties are achieved by creating a reference and blessing it. Please note that a blessed reference is an object. There's nothing more to it. However, we will have to write our own constructor that will create this blessed reference. There's no 'this' keyword in Perl. The class name or blessed reference is passed as first argument.

Following is a code sample of what such a class would look like:

```
package Whatever;
use strict;
use warnings;
sub new {
  my $self  = {
  # List of properties are defined here
  }
  bless $self, 'Whatever';
  return $self;
}
```

All this is just to get a mere working implementation of a class. Now, what does it take to ensure our class uses some of the best practices established by OO? For example, if we had to implement encapsulation and want only setters for certain properties. More so, what if we would like to validate the data for each of these properties before setting them? You can imagine, we will have to write a function for setting and getting the value and implement the validation logic, if any. Yes, there are CPAN modules that do this automatically. Yet, creating well-implemented classes are not that friendly. Having the liberty to implement the properties of our own class leaves room for so much flexibility. Following is an explanation of how Moose addresses the challenges above without necessarily destroying the flexibility.

OO in Moose

We will discover in this chapter how Moose simplifies the process.

Properties

When using Moose, a property can be implemented by just saying:

```
has 'propertyname' => (
   is => '[rw|ro|bare]',
   isa => '[datatype]'
)
```

Note: Normal parenthesis.

As shown, the syntax is very declarative and one has to only say that the class **has** a certain property and **is** readable or writable or both and that it **is a** string or integer type or whatever predefined or custom data type you want it to be!

Class method

Defining methods in Perl has always been only declaring the subroutine. So Moose does not have much to offer here. However, Moose offers what are known as method modifiers. **Method modifiers** are subroutines that need to be executed before, after, or around the execution of the method itself. This feature is especially important for inheritance and other hierarchy design principles. For example:

```
sub runfast
{

}
```

is a method. Please note that the () would be an empty prototype, which doesn't make sense on a method.

Following could be before and after modifiers applied to the method:

```
before 'runfast'  => sub {
   print "Warm up First";
};
after 'runfast' => sub {
   print "Cool Down";
};
```

Instantiating objects

Moose provides a `new()` method for every package, which can be used as a constructor. The flexibility that comes with writing your own constructors in Perl is still available by defining a `BUILD` method. The `BUILD` method is called for any manipulation immediately after Moose creates the new object. You do not need to use method modifiers or other means of calling a parent class' `BUILD` method. Moose will automatically call all `BUILD` methods in the hierarchy in the correct order.

Inheritance

Moose makes inheritance simple, which is illustrated in the following code:

```
Package Creation;
Use Moose;
#Some Code Here
Package Human
Use Moose;
extends 'Creation';
```

Now this class can make use of properties and methods from `Creation`.

All that has to be said is class child `extends` parents.

An interesting concept that Moose introduces is called roles. Roles are encapsulated behavior. Roles as we will explore later will make the creation of plugins in Catalyst simpler. Roles are not classes, so they cannot be instantiated. However, they (the properties and methods the package defines) can be used by other classes or roles. You can think of roles as abstract classes or interfaces. Abstract classes or interfaces are classes that can't be used directly but define methods that classes inheriting them should implement. This is illustrated in the following code example:

```
Package Creation;
Use Moose::Role;
Requires 'sensoryinput';
Package Human;
Use Moose;
with 'Creation';
# Now this class has to define sensoryinput as it uses the role
creation
sub sensoryinput {
  #some code
}
```

The last code example is a summary of most commonly used OO concepts and its syntax in Moose. This by no means is a primer on Moose; however, this will help you to quickly relate to some of the text covered later. However, I recommend learning to use Moose and its fundamentals. There is a Moose cookbook on cpan. Also, I find the following links interesting and a quick refresher on Moose, especially if you have read the other Perl OO tutorials such as perlboot at:

```
http://www.stonehenge.com/merlyn/LinuxMag/col94.html
```

```
http://www.stonehenge.com/merlyn/LinuxMag/col95.html
```

Moose in Catalyst

The moosified version of our application (`AddressBook.pm`) from the previous chapter will look like the following code sample. You will need to moosify your application if you want to use any moosified plugin/role in your application.

```
package AddressBook;
use Moose;
use namespace::autoclean;
use Catalyst( qw/
  ConfigLoader
  Static::Simple
/);
$app->config( name => 'MyApp' );
$app->setup;
# If you want to make use of modifiers. You can do something like this
before finalize
{
  # Do something here before the finalize of every response
};
```

As discussed earlier, `before` is the modifier and we can just ask Catalyst to run the last code before executing the `finalize` method.

The use of `namespace::autoclean` is a best practice, which cleans up the imported functions from the namespace.

Controller

Moose can be used in the Catalyst controllers to make use of method modifiers like we just did. This is demonstrated in the following code sample with a controller method we had written in Chapter 6:

```
package AddressBook::Controller::Test;
use Moose;
use namespace::autoclean;
BEGIN { extends 'Catalyst::Controller' };
sub count_users : Local {
  my ($self, $c) = @_;
  my $count = $c->model('AddressDBI')->count_users();
  $c->stash->{message}="There are $count users. ";
}
after count_users => sub {
  $c->stash->{message} .= "And they all Like Moose");
};
```

The last code is a simple example of using Moose in a controller. Just like in the application package, we use `Moose` and `namespace::autoclean`. We use `extends 'Catalyst::Controller'` just as explained in how Moose allows inheritance. The `extends` is wrapped in a `BEGIN` block, so the parent is declared as soon as Perl sees the line. This makes sure that the subroutine attributes such as `:Local` can be resolved at compile time.

The example uses the `after` method modifier to effectively execute a block of code after the execution of the method `count_users`.

CatalystX declare

Catalyst declare is an experimental plugin that can make the application, controller, and model description more descriptive and easier. It is not really a plugin, but rather a declarative syntax module based on `Devel::Declare`. It is a specialized version of `MooseX-Declare`.

Also, note that `CatalystX-Declare` will probably change it's behavior in the future a bit, as it really is experimental.

The last example using `Catalyst::Declare` can be rewritten as follows:

```
Use CatalystX::Declare
controller AddressBook::Controller::Test;
action count_users as 'count' under '/'  {
  my $count = $ctx->model('AddressDBI')->count_users();
```

```
    $ctx->stash->{message}="There are $count users. ";
}
after count_users {
    $ctx->stash->{message} .= "And they all Like Moose");
}
```

 The method modifiers are parsed by MooseX-Declare, and therefore, are also a syntax element and not in the procedural around foo => sub { } form. There's also no need to access the arguments directly. $self and $ctx are automatically lexically available, and all other parameters can be defined in the signature as with MooseX-Declare.

At first glance it doesn't look like much. However, once you understand the changes in declaration above, you will be taken through the benefits. As you can notice, using CatalystX::Declare makes a few changes to the way controller and controller methods are defined. The controller itself is defined using the controller keyword and actions are defined using the action.

Please note that actions are defined with action, methods are defined with method as follows.

```
action count_users as 'count' under '/'
```

The last line means that this controller method will be executed when the query path is the following controllerpath/count. Notice that it mentions that the name of the controller method is count and the name of the method follows the "/" immediately.

If you are already beginning to wonder if this is similar to the chaining syntax that you have learned earlier, then you are right! CatalystX::Declare simplifies chaining for method declaration. So the following line:

```
action count_users as 'count' under '/'
```

is the equivalent of the following line:

```
sub count_users: Chained('/') PathPart('count')  CaptureArgs(0)
```

As you can see, CatalystX::Declare already provides value in being more descriptive on the chaining syntax. But that's not all. Consider a chaining situation where the base action is the same and there are many chained items. We can achieve that easily by:

```
Final action customers under base { #Block code goes here }
Final action vendors under base { #Block code goes here }
```

Or

```
under count {
  final action customers { #Block code goes here }
  final action  vendors {#Block code goes here }
}
```

If this had to be written using the regular Perl syntax it would have been:

```
sub count_users: Chained('count') PathPart('customers') CaptureArgs(0)
{ # Block code goes here }
sub count_users: Chained('count') PathPart('vendors') CaptureArgs(0)
{ #Block code goes here }
```

`CatalystX::Declare` also provides a mechanism for method signatures. That is, `CatalystX::Declare` makes it possible to define the arguments that a method expects in a declarative syntax.

For example, the `vendors` method can expect a vendor ID and hence can be written as follows:

```
Final action vendors under base (Int $id ) { #Block code goes here  }
```

As shown with the usage of **is a** earlier, there are defined types already and it is also simple to define your own data types. Having `Int $id` will pass any integer after the action's path part in the URL to the controller action.

Hence, the URL `Test/count/vendors/12` will execute the above method passing 12 as the parameter. However, `Test/count/vendors/abcd` will not call this method.

Having method signatures allows for a behavior very similar to method overriding. Suppose, you would like to accept either an ID or a name for the above method and have two different procedures for handling those parameters. You would do something like the following:

```
Final action vendors_id as vendors under base (Int id ) { #code goes
here  }
Final action vendors_name as vendors under base (String id ) { #code
goes here   }
```

The previous statements will result in the following URLs: `Test/count/vendors/12` executing the `vendors_id` block and `Test/count/vendors/abcd` executing the `vendors_name` block.

Of course, this is just an example to demonstrate the concept. There are better uses of this functionality when abstracted carefully. For further reading on `CatalystX::Declare` refer to the following two links:

```
http://search.cpan.org/~phaylon/CatalystX-Declare-0.011/lib/
CatalystX/Declare.pm
```

```
http://www.catalystframework.org/calendar/2009/5
```

CatalystX

You may have been wondering about the namespace **CatalystX**. Well CatalystX is the namespace used by Catalyst modules that extend Catalyst but are neither plugins nor typical Catalyst components. Available Catalyst packages include a variety of functionalities that can make your application development easier by reusing code. For a complete list of modules, search for CatalystX on cpan:

```
http://search.cpan.org/search?m=all&q=catalystx&s=71
```

You may also want to explore `CatalystX::Traits`, which are loadable Moose roles that can be used in your application—model, controller, and view. To understand more on this read `http://www.catalystframework.org/calendar/2009/10`.

For an example of traits, you may want to have a look at the CatalystX SimpleLogin trait at:

```
http://search.cpan.org/~bobtfish/CatalystX-SimpleLogin-0.09/lib/
CatalystX/SimpleLogin.pm
```

Roles

The `with` keyword that we have discussed above allows easy use of Moose roles in a Catalyst application.

Following is an example of using roles in a controller:

```
use Moose;
use namespace::autoclean;
BEGIN { extends 'Catalyst::Controller' };
with 'MyApp::ControllerRole';
```

To define a role you can use the following syntax:

```
package MyApp::ControllerRole;
use MooseX::MethodAttributes::Role;
use namespace::autoclean;
```

Note that this role is similar to any other class except that it uses `MooseX::`
`MethodAttributes::Role` instead of Moose. This is a Moose extension that
allows roles to provide subroutine attributes that will be composed into the
consuming class.

Traits are similar to roles except that they are applied to the objects and not the class.
What this means is that the meta of any object will access the elements in the class.

For example look at the following code:

```
package MyApp::Meta::Class::Trait::SomeClass;
use Moose::Role;
sub foo { warn 'foo' }
package Moose::Meta::Class::Custom::Trait::SomeClass;
sub register_implementation { 'MyApp::Meta::Class::Trait::HasTable' }
package MyApp::User;
use Moose -traits => 'HasTable';
__PACKAGE__->meta->foo();
```

You can see that traits are used similar to roles here, except that the meta (class
details) of the package is used to access the methods. You can think of this as
dynamically applied roles.

Traits makes a lot of things very simple. You may want to explore more about
loadable traits and using them with controllers and many such things once you
get familiar with Moose. A good read is `http://www.catalystframework.org/`
`calendar/2009/10`.

Traits really exploit the meta programming capability that Moose brings at your
disposal. More on meta programming and Moose can be read at `http://search.`
`cpan.org/~flora/Moose-1.07/lib/Moose/Cookbook/Meta/Recipe2.pod`

Types

In this section, we will briefly discuss data types as mentioned previously. You are
already aware that there are a collection of predefined data types that can be used
with *isa* when declaring a property or with a method parameter when using `Catalyst`
`Declare`. In this section, we will learn how to define our own data types. Let us start
with a well-written example from the `MooseX::Types` definition (refer to `http://`
`search.cpan.org/~rkitover/MooseX-Types-0.21/lib/MooseX/Types.pm`):

```
subtype PositiveInt,
as Int,
where { $_ >= 0 },
message { "Int is not larger than 0" };
```

Include 0, otherwise the coercion defined below won't work. Because 0 * -1 is still 0 and wouldn't pass.

In the last example, a `PositiveInt` type is created as a subtype of `Int`. The constraint for the type is provided by the `where` block, which in this example checks if the passed argument is greater than `0` for `PositiveInt`. The `message` block describes the error message that is returned on failing the type constraint.

Any type or subtype creates the following additional exports:

Is_type:

The `is_type` accessor checks if the given argument is of a particular type. For example, `is_PostiveInt(10);`

To_Type:

The `to_type` accessor does typecasting or coerces one type to another. Note that Moose uses the term coercion for the transformation from one type to another. For example, `to_PositiveInt(-10).`

However, to make use of `to_type`, the type must have a coerce declaration as follows:

```
coerce PositiveInt,
from Int,
via {  abs $_ };
```

The above argument will take any negative number and covert it to positive by multiplying it with -1 which is defined within the `via` block. The typecast, however, works works only for integers and hence we have restricted coercing to `Int` using `from`.

Being able to declare transitions of values from one form to another outside of the classes that use them is a very powerful form of encapsulation. There are also lots of `MooseX-Types` libraries already on CPAN handling things such as DateTime, URI and Path::Class values among many others.

Model

Moose can potentially offer a lot of value when working with models. An ideal mechanism would be to combine the features of `Moose` with `DBIx::Class`. Though work is under way to integrate both, at the time of writing this to leverage the power of DBIC and Moose, the declarations have to be made twice in the model.

The advantage of declaring attributes using Moose along with DBIC in the model is that the attributes can benefit from type checking with "isa". At this stage you may not find many benefits with this approach. However, if you would like to see an example, you may want to follow the link `http://code2.0beta.co.uk/reaction/svn/Reaction/0.001/trunk/t/lib/RTest/TestDB/Foo.pm`.

Immutable

The last thing that you will have to be aware of is that the Moose definitions of methods and properties and even the class can change at runtime. However, in most cases this flexibility is not required. Informing Moose that your class will not go mutation at runtime can save on some performance. Hence, it is always a good practice to end your Moose classes with the following line:

```
__PACKAGE__->meta->make_immutable(inline_constructor => 0);
```

The `inline_constructor => 0` is only required if you are inheriting from a non-Moose class that defines its own constructor. You might also want to use `MooseX::NonMoose` in that case, as that will upgrade the original constructor and make sure that things such as `BUILD` are called, attributes are initialized, and so on.

Summary

In this chapter, we examined how Moose can make declarations of methods and properties simpler in our application. We examined how chained controllers can be easily defined with `CatalystX::Declare`. We also discovered what Moose allows for property constraints along with best practices. Also, remember to read and learn more on Moose from the cookbook at `http://search.cpan.org/dist/Moose/lib/Moose/Manual.pod`. What is covered in this chapter is merely an introduction.

Please note that Moose itself is pure Perl; it doesn't have method signatures. If you want those, you will have to use `MooseX-Declare` or `MooseX-Method-Signatures`.

9
Deployment

At some point in your application's lifecycle, you're going to run the application on a machine other than your development environment. In this chapter we'll cover packaging your application (for internal or CPAN release) and running that package in a production environment with a real web server. As many deployment options can change from time to time, you can check `http://wiki.catalystframework. org/wiki/deployment` for up-to-date deployment information.

Basics

The first step in deploying your application is to copy your application from your development/build environment to your production environment. This may sound trivial, but it's important to make sure that your process is easy and repeatable. If you require every step to be done manually, it's likely that at some point (under the pressure of short maintenance windows), something will be missed and your users will be unhappy. Are you sure you remembered to install every dependency, update the source tree on every server in the farm, change permissions, and edit configuration files appropriately?

Fortunately, Catalyst makes it easy to carry out the deployment correctly. If you've been diligent about keeping the dependencies in your `Makefile.PL` up-to-date, then you'll find it very easy to manage dependencies and the application itself.

Let's start with a quick run-through of the `Makefile.PL` build process. We will use `Makefile.PL` twice, once on the build system (to build the package) and again on the target system, to build the application itself.

The first step is to run `Makefile.PL` on your development or build system as follows:

```
$ perl Makefile.PL
```

This will generate a `Makefile` that includes some useful targets—`make dist`, `make test`, `make clean`, `make manifest`, `make distclean`, and many others. Before we build a distribution, we'll want to run `make distclean` to delete any non-code that has accumulated during the development process. Unfortunately, as the `Makefile` is considered a temporary file, it will be removed in this step. After the `distclean`, re-run `Makefile.PL` to regenerate the `Makefile`.

Now that you have a clean working directory, you can generate a `manifest` file containing a list of the files in your application. `make manifest` will do this automatically and save the results in a file called `MANIFEST`. If this file looks good, you're ready for the next step. If it contains entries that aren't a part of your application, then create a file called `MANIFEST.SKIP` to indicate paths to skip. A `MANIFEST.SKIP` that I usually use looks like this:

```
.git/
blib
pm_to_blib
MANIFEST.bak
MANIFEST.SKIP~
cover_db
Makefile$
Makefile.old$
```

The format is one regular expression per line. If a file's full path is matched by any regular expression in the file, then it will be skipped over when building the manifest.

You can test the skip list by re-running `make manifest`. That command will inform you of what it added to, or removed from the manifest based on the new skip rules.

When the manifest is to your liking, all that's left to do is to actually build the package with `make dist`. The `make dist` command will build a compressed TAR file of your application called `MyApp-0.01.tar.gz` that contains the source (and `Makefile.PL`) of your application, suitable for uploading to the CPAN or copying to another system to install. The 0.01 in the filename is the version number that can be changed by editing the `our $VERSION = '0.01'` line in your application's main file, `lib/MyApp.pm`. Traditionally, versions start at 0.01 and are increased by 0.01 on each release. Test releases are marked with a version number, an underscore, and another number, such as 0.01_01 (note that 0.01_01 sorts after 0.01). Many utilities assume this convention, so it's good to stick to it even if you don't plan to release your code to the world.

With this package built, the final step is to copy the tarball to your deployment server. On that machine, simply run:

```
$ tar xzvf MyApp-0.01.tar.gz
$ cd MyApp
$ perl Makefile.PL
$ make && make test
```

That will extract the application, generate the `Makefile`, install all the dependencies that `Makefile.PL` mentions and finally, run the application's automated test suite. If all goes well, you're ready to point your web server at the application directory.

PAR deployment

If your build environment and production are at the same platform, you can save some time and trouble by deploying a PAR package instead of manually building a tarball. A PAR file is a Perl Archive, a self-contained Perl application. It will contain your application and all the dependencies, which means that you can copy a single file to all of your production machines and have your application "Just Work".

Building a PAR is usually as simple as adding a line that says:

```
catalyst_par();
```

to your `Makefile.PL`, running `Makefile.PL`, and then running `make catalyst_par`. The PAR packer will examine your application to determine its dependencies and then generate an archive that bundles the dependencies, your application, and the scripts to run the application together in a file called `myapp.par`. To run your application, put the PAR file somewhere convenient and then run `parl myapp.par <script>`, where the script is `myapp_server.pl`, `myapp_fastcgi.pl`, `myapp_test.pl`, and so on. The PAR will unpack itself and then execute the requested command.

Note that the command is `parl`, not Perl; it's included in the PAR CPAN distribution, which must be installed on the target system.

Sometimes the auto-scanning of your application might not pick up all the dependencies; you can manually add a list of dependencies to always include, by including the following line inside `Makefile.PL`:

```
catalyst_par_classes(qw/A::Dependency Another::Dependency .../);
```

Configuration management

It's likely that your development and production environments will require different configuration files. Catalyst provides a few ways to handle this. The most flexible is to maintain separate configuration files for each instance of your application (development, staging, QA, production, and so on) and set the `MYAPP_CONFIG` environment variable to point to the correct file on each environment.

If there is a lot of configuration that overlaps between the instances, then that approach might not be ideal. Catalyst has a concept of local configuration files that you can use instead. If there is an environment variable called `MYAPP_CONFIG_LOCAL_SUFFIX` set, then Catalyst will supplement the default configuration (say, `myapp.yml`) with a file named `myapp_<suffix>.yml`. The default suffix is local, so if you have only two environments to configure, then you can put your development-specific settings in the local file and simply copy the `myapp_local.yml` file to production.

If you have more than two environments, put the bulk of your config in `myapp.yml`, then create a `myapp_envname.yml` for each environment. Then just set the `MYAPP_CONFIG_LOCAL_SUFFIX` environment variable appropriately, and you're set.

 If you use the hostname as the suffix, you can say `MYAPP_CONFIG_LOCAL_SUFFIX='hostname';` then even the environment variable setting is identical between machines.

Alternatively, you can specify configuration directly as environment variables with the `Catalyst::Plugin::ConfigLoader::Environment` extension.

Configuring a web server

Once you have your application working on the production machine, you're ready to point a real web server at it. Which server you use is usually decided by what your other applications are using. If you already have Apache and mod_perl set up, then use that. If you aren't serving many users, you will probably be fine with just the development server included with Catalyst. If you're tired of Apache, you can use lighttpd with FastCGI. Catalyst tries to make mod_perl, FastCGI, and the development server behave the same, so you should use whatever is convenient for you. (Note that plain CGI is also an option, but it will be unbearably slow, so don't use it.)

Generally, new deployments use Apache and FastCGI, as that configuration is relatively easy to set up and manage. As of writing, this FastCGI is the preferred configuration and unless you have reasons otherwise, you probably should just stick with FastCGI. mod_perl is most useful if you want to write an Apache module integrating Perl code directly into the web server. For applications, FastCGI is simpler to set up and manage in the usual cases.

Apache

Apache is the world's most common web server, so most sites are already using Apache and have a configuration that you can easily add to your Catalyst application. If you decide to use Apache, you can use either mod_perl or FastCGI to actually run your Catalyst application.

FastCGI

FastCGI is easiest of the two to set up; simply install mod_fastcgi (or the newer mod_fcgid, which might be better for some users) and add the following to Apache's `httpd.conf` file:

```
FastCgiServer /.../myapp/script/myapp_fastcgi.pl -processes 3
Alias /myapp/ /.../myapp/script/myapp_fastcgi.pl/
```

 Please note that in the last lines of code, the ellipsis (...) is an abbreviation for wherever you want your application code to live. Many sites use `/var/www` or `/var/www-apps`, but `/home/myapp/` or something similar is also possible.

The Apache configuration may look like the following on a virtual host:

```
<VirtualHost *:80>
  AddHandler fastcgi-script .fcgi
  ServerName myapp.com
  ServerAlias www.myapp.com
  DocumentRoot /mnt/volume/www/myapp/root
  FastCgiServer /mnt/volume/www/myapp/script/myapp_fastcgi.pl -
    processes 1
  Alias /static/ /mnt/volume/www/myapp/root/static/
  Alias / /mnt/volume/www/myapp/script/myapp_fastcgi.pl/
  <Location /mnt/volume/www/myapp/root/static/>
    SetHandler default-handler
  </Location>
</VirtualHost>
```

For more details on setting up fastcgi on Apache, you can read `http://httpd.apache.org/mod_fcgid/`.

This configuration will tell Apache to start (and maintain) three instances of your application, and to make the application available on the web under the `/myapp` URL. You can put the `Alias` directive inside a `VirtualHost` block to make your application available at the root of a virtual host.

If you'd like to run your FastCGI server on a separate machine, you can tell Apache about a FastCGI external server:

```
FastCgiExternalServer /var/www/htdocs/myapp.fcgi -host remote.server.
com:3010
Alias /myapp/ /var/www/htdocs/myapp.fcgi
```

Note that `/var/www/htdocs/myapp.fcgi` isn't a real file; it's a virtual file that ends with `.fcgi` (so Apache knows to invoke the fastcgi-handler) and exists inside the doc root (so Apache knows it's allowed to be served). The `-host` directive points FastCGI at the server running on `remote.server.com`, port 3010.

On `remote.server.com`, you'll want to run `scripts/myapp_fastcgi.pl -l :3010` and set up firewall rules so that only your frontend server can talk to port 3010. You can also use another port number, as there is no defined standard port.

If your application is in a PAR, you can start an external FastCGI server by running `parl myapp.par myapp_fastcgi.pl -l :3010`. You can then configure a remote Apache with FastCGI to support to connect to that server, just as described above for the non-PAR case.

In addition, the external server need not be on another host, it can be run on localhost the same way. You can also use a named socket on the filesystem instead of a host and port; just say `-socket` instead of `-host`. It is easier to enforce permissions on files than TCP ports, so if you care about fine-grained access to the FastCGI server, then you might like using the named socket better. Keep in mind that you can't use a named socket when the FastCGI server is running on a different host from the frontend web server.

Static content

One last tweak is to have Apache serve your static content without involving your Catalyst application. All you'll need to do is add an `Alias` directive like the following:

```
Alias /myapp/static /.../myapp/root/static
```

Apache can serve static content much more efficiently than your Catalyst application, so for maximum performance it's best to add this piece of configuration.

mod_perl

For years, mod_perl was the only way to write efficient web applications, so it's still in wide use. Serving your Catalyst application with mod_perl is very easy. First, you'll need `Catalyst::Engine::Apache` from the CPAN.

Then, to a mod_perl-enabled Apache 2.x.x configuration, you'll just need to add the following lines:

```
PerlSwitches -I/.../myapp/lib
PerlModule MyApp
<Location /> # or you can use /myapp, or a VirtualHost, etc.
  SetHandler modperl
  PerlResponseHandler MyApp
</Location>
```

On Apache 1.3, the setup is slightly different:

```
<Perl>
  use lib qw(/.../myapp/lib);
</Perl> PerlModule MyApp
<Location />
  SetHandler perl-script
  PerlHandler MyApp
</Location>
```

Finally, if you're using PAR, you can install `Apache::PAR` and point Apache at the PAR instead of a directory:

```
PerlAddVar PARInclude /.../myapp.par
PerlModule Apache::PAR
PerlModule MyApp
```

These directives replace the `<Perl>` or `PerlSwitches` sections (but not the `<Location>` section).

After you have set up your configuration, you can restart Apache and enjoy your application. The same static caveat with FastCGI applies to mod_perl, so you will want to add an alias or location for serving the static content directly. (This is more difficult with PAR, but you might want to take the slight performance hit for the convenience of one-file deployment. Additionally, you can copy the static content somewhere outside of the PAR file and use only the PAR for code. Then there is no performance hit, but maintenance is slightly more difficult.)

Performance considerations

Unfortunately, the mod_perl setup described in the previous section is not ideal. mod_perl works by loading your entire application into every Apache process. This means that when an Apache process has to spoon-feed a dial-up user a 200M movie (or 20k of HTML, the concept is the same), the memory that your application used is wasted streaming bytes instead of processing requests. On sites with high traffic, this will result in unacceptable performance, as the application processes will be tied up serving data (and you can't start more application processes because you'll be out of memory).

This is a well-known mod_perl problem not specific to Catalyst (or even Perl, mod_ruby, and mod_python suffer the same problem), and is part of the reason why FastCGI is becoming popular.

The solution is to run a two-tiered architecture. In front of your mod_perl application processes, you place a lean load balancer (such as perlbal) or a basic Apache process. The frontend will pass dynamic requests to the backend application servers. When the dynamic result is ready, the dynamic server will send it very quickly to the frontend server. The frontend server will then send the response to the client. While that frontend server is tied up, another lean frontend server can dispatch another dynamic request to your application. This setup ensures that you are always using as much CPU and bandwidth as possible.

Setting up a frontend server is covered in the mod_perl book at `http://perl.apache.org/`, and perlbal is covered in the next section. The only thing you need to do for Catalyst is to tell it that there's a frontend proxy by setting `using_frontend_proxy` to `1` in the application config. This option is necessary so that Catalyst will generate URLs that point to the frontend server when you use `uri_for` and `uri_for_action`.

If you're going to use mod_perl for a large site, be sure to set up a two-tiered architecture.

Development server and perlbal

The final deployment option is to simply use the `myapp_server.pl` development server. This server is not intrinsically limited in any way; you can expose it to the Internet and your application will work fine. The main problem is the same as mod_perl, though; feeding the resulting HTML (or images, and so on) back to the client will tie up system memory unnecessarily. Additionally, as the development server can handle only one connection at a time, users will have to wait in line to use your application, which is probably not acceptable unless you are creating something like a desktop web application.

That means it's easy to get a very efficient two-tiered setup going with perlbal. The basic idea is to start a pool of development servers running on different ports, and then have perlbal load balance between them. perlbal will handle talking to clients and will send dynamic requests to a waiting development server. The performance of this setup will be excellent, as perlbal adds almost no overhead (it's used for popular sites such LiveJournal and Vox, and easily handles hundreds of millions of requests a day).

To get started, install perlbal from the CPAN (it's also available at `http://www.danga.com/perlbal/`). Then, create a simple perlbal configuration file called `/etc/perlbal/perlbal.conf` that looks like this:

```
CREATE POOL myapp
POOL myapp ADD 127.0.0.1:3010
POOL myapp ADD 127.0.0.1:3011
POOL myapp ADD 127.0.0.1:3012
POOL myapp ADD 127.0.0.1:3013
CREATE SERVICE balancer
SET listen = 0.0.0.0:80
SET role = reverse_proxy
SET pool = myapp
SET persist_client = on
SET persist_backend = on
ENABLE balancer
# open up a management port for dynamic configuration
CREATE SERVICE mgmt
SET role = management
SET listen = 127.0.0.1:60000
ENABLE mgmt
```

When that's set up, start a few instances of your application:

```
$ perl script/myapp_server.pl -p 3010 -d
$ perl script/myapp_server.pl -p 3011 -d
$ perl script/myapp_server.pl -p 3012 -d
$ perl script/myapp_server.pl -p 3013 -d
```

and start perlbal:

```
$ perlbal
```

Now visit `http://localhost/`, and you should be good to go. If you choose to keep perlbal's management interface up, you should firewall off its port (60000).

Database

Storage and schema deployment, upgrade, and maintenance could be a major challenge if not handled with care. You may want to explore the class DBIx::Class::Schema::Versioned that helps with schema versioning. Refer to

http://search.cpan.org/~ash/DBIx-Class-0.08013/lib/DBIx/Class/Schema/Versioned.pm.

Versioning code

If you do not know already, it is always a good practice to version control your code. A **version control system** (**VCS**) brings in the following benefits:

- You can go back in time and check any code
- Allow multiple developers to work on the same code base and manage conflicts
- Document changes to specific code releases/commits
- Easier management of production code updates.

There are many VCS available. I personally recommend using **Git**.

You can read more about Git at http://git-scm.com/documentation.

Following is a quick summary on the basics of Git:

Initializing

Once you have created a Catalyst application or any folder that you want to version control, you need to first initialize it as a Git repository. This can be done with git init.

Adding files

After you initialize a repository, you have to add the files that you want to version control. This is called adding files to the repository. You can add files using git add. Generally, it is standard practice to use git add to add all files to the repository recursively.

Committing changes

After making any changes to the files in the repository, you can use git commit to commit those changes to the repository. You may want to use git add filename first if you have made changes to a file that was not tracked, if there is more than one developer or if you are developing on more than one machine.

Getting another working repository

You can get a copy of a repository in which you can make changes and commit by using the `git clone` command as follows:

```
git clone pathtorepository
```

If you are familiar with VCS, you may want to know that in Git, every cloned folder is a repository as it is a distributed VCS.

Getting updates

You can get the latest commits from a repository using the `git pull` command. `git pull` gets the update from the repository from which it was cloned. However, as you will learn when using Git, it is possible to pull updates from any repository or even to fetch only particular commits by cherrypicking!

Pushing changes

Once you have made some commits in repository, you can push these changes to another repository with `git push`. Similar to `git pull` you can push to any repository.

You may want to read more on checkout, branching, tagging, and other concepts to use Git more efficiently. Whenever working on a project always use a version control system.

Summary

In this chapter, we moved our application from development to production. We learned how `Makefile.PL` made it simple to manage dependencies and create packages. We also saw how to create a unique configuration for each environment, and how to set up a variety of web servers. We learned how to make our application a self-contained file, called a PAR. We also learned how to version database and code for easy maintenance and deployment.

10
Testing

Automatic testing is an important part of any programming project. It's always good to know that your application works correctly, but it's tedious to manually click through your application's interface every time you change something. Automatic testing transfers this burden onto the computer; after you've written the tests, the application will test itself whenever necessary. Thus, adding new features becomes a low risk operation because your tests will start failing as soon as you break something; you'll be able to fix the problem immediately, and you won't have to worry about the fix breaking something else. If your tests are well written, you can spend your time adding features, rather than tracking down obscure bugs at 3 A.M.

While this book doesn't intend to push any development methodology, there are a few schools of thinking on when to write tests. One is called **test-driven development (TDD)**, which suggests that you always write tests before you write any code. The idea is that before adding a feature you run your test suite, notice that everything passes, and then add some failing tests. Then you write the code until the tests go green, and you repeat the process for the next feature. When all the features are implemented, you also have a fully-tested application, as no code can be written without writing a test first. This is an easy way to ensure that all of your code is tested; you're simply not allowed to implement a feature until it's tested. You won't have to worry about not having enough time to test something before release—if the feature is working, it's also tested. This is generally good, which is why the movement has attracted so much positive attention.

The other end of the spectrum is waiting until your application is completely built before you write tests. Although it looks like we're doing this in the book, I actually wrote the tests along with the code but saved them until this chapter so that they would get enough text to explain them adequately. I don't recommend that you try this for your real applications. Writing tests is a development aid, so waiting until development is complete misses much of the point of testing. The tests will be helpful for the next development cycle, but you still probably wasted a lot of time in this cycle by manually doing what the computer could do for you. So, get disciplined and write tests as you develop the code the first time.

Even though it seems like you're wasting time by not writing application code, you'll find that in the end you save time, and you won't lose sleep wondering what your last commit broke.

I prefer a hybrid approach to writing tests. I try to write as many tests as possible for a component or feature before I start writing a code for it, but I don't make any effort to be sure that I've got every case that I'm going to write the code for. Then, I code for a bit, and test the basic flow of the application through the interface, just to make sure that I didn't do anything too stupid (such as typos). Once I'm sure that the application doesn't contain any obvious errors, I write tests for the corner cases and fix the errors in the code without using the interface at all. If a bug comes up later, I'll experiment a bit to reproduce the bug, add a test to the appropriate error, and then try to make the test pass without wasting time with the web interface.

As you get familiar with testing, you'll find a style that works well for you. If this chapter is your first exposure to automated testing, I recommend that you try the TDD methodology. After a while, you'll know when you don't need to strictly adhere to the procedure, but in the mean time, you'll be writing tested code at a pretty good pace.

In this chapter, we'll take a look at the technologies and techniques available to make testing your Catalyst application easy. We'll start by seeing how to run the autogenerated tests, and where to put new ones. Then, we'll begin testing ChatStat by testing the data model outside of Catalyst. After that, we'll write a few tests to ensure that the web interface is working well with the data model. Then, we'll write some tests for the AddressBook application. After reading the chapter, it is important that you take time to understand the testing culture and the various modules in CPAN carefully. Many common use cases are already available and you do not have to reinvent the wheel. Always continually explore and discover ways to make testing more efficient and fun!

Mechanics

Before we start writing tests, let's take a look at what we have so far. Out of the box, your Catalyst application already has a few tests in the `t/` directory of the application. You can run these by making a Makefile with `Makefile.PL` as follows:

```
$ perl Makefile.PL

<output>

$ make test t/01app.................ok t/02pod................skipped

all skipped: set TEST_POD to enable this test t/03podcoverage.........
skipped
```

```
all skipped: set TEST_POD to enable this test t/controller_Address....ok
```

```
t/controller_Person.....ok t/model_AddressDB.......ok t/view_
Jemplate.........ok
```

```
All tests successful, 2 tests skipped.
```

```
Files=7, Tests=9, 3 wallclock secs ( 2.92 cusr + 0.29 csys =  3.21 CPU)
```

The tests you see running here were added by `catalyst.pl` (the ones that start with numbers), or by the `addressbook_create.pl` script (the ones that start with Model and View). These tests don't really do much testing, because they're just autogenerated tests that see if the code compiles. Here's what the `t/view_Jemplate.t` looks like:

```
use strict;
use warnings;
use Test::More tests => 1;
BEGIN { use_ok 'AddressBook::View::Jemplate' }
```

Although this test doesn't do much, it does show the structure of a test file. A test is just a Perl script that ends with a `.t` extension. We use the strict and warnings pragmas, and then use a module called `Test::More`. `Test::More` produces an output that can be read by a module called `Test::Harness`. This is what makes test uses to generate the summary above. If you run the tests manually, the output looks like the following:

```
$ perl -Ilib t/view_Jemplate.t
1..1
ok 1 - use AddressBook::View::Jemplate;
```

This output format is called **TAP (Test Anything Protocol)**, and is generated for you by `Test::More`. Although you could generate TAP manually, it's easier to just let the module do it for you.

One last note—Perl comes with a command called `prove` that will do the same thing as `make test`:

```
$ prove -Ilib t/view_Jemplate.t t/view_Jemplate....ok
All tests successful.
Files=1, Tests=1, 0 wallclock secs ( 0.20 cusr + 0.02 csys = 0.22 CPU)
```

The command `prove` is nice when you only want to run a few test files instead of the entire suite.

Testing ChatStat

Now that we have seen what tests look like and how to run them, let's dive into testing ChatStat. When I was first writing ChatStat, I designed it with testability in mind. The key practice here is to make as many components of the application work as possible without depending on other parts of the application. Testing a Perl class is very easy, but firing up a Catalyst application and testing it by making requests and looking at the HTML is hard. So, I tried to keep the need for the second type of test down by not doing much inside Catalyst. All the hard stuff is inside the easily-testable Perl modules. This not only makes testing easy, it's just a plain good design. Without any effort on my part, I can use the same code to write a command-line version of the application, or perhaps an IRC interface.

Let's get started by writing some tests for the ChatStat message parser. This isn't particularly related to the Catalyst part of the application, but if this doesn't work, the whole application is useless. In addition, this is the simplest test to write, so it's a good practice before we move on to more complex parts of the application.

We'll start with a very simple test for the parse_nickname function, located in the ChatStat::Robot::Parser module from *Chapter 5, Building a More Advanced Application*. This function takes a string like person!~username@some-host.com and produces an array like ['person', 'username', 'some-host.com'].

In t/irc-parser-nickname.t, add the following:

```
use strict;
use warnings;
use Test::More; qw/no_plan/
use ChatStat::Robot::Parser;
my %tests = (
  # me @ example.com
  'jrockway!~jrockway@example.com' => ['jrockway', 'jrockway',
    'example.com']
);
plan tests => scalar keys %tests;
while (my ($k, $v) = each %tests) {
  my $get = [parse_nickname($k)];
  my $expect = $v;
  is_deeply($get, $expect, "$k parses");
}
```

We wrote this test by creating a table at the top of the test with the input string and the expected output result. Then we told Test::More how many tests we're going to run (so it can warn us if the test file dies halfway through), and finally we run parse_nickname on each input and used the is_deeply function in Test::More to see if the data we got and the expected data was the same.

You can try running the test with `prove` as follows:

```
$ prove -Ilib t/irc-parser-nickname.t t/irc-parser-nickname....ok
All tests successful.
Files=1, Tests=1, 0 wallclock secs ( 0.12 cusr + 0.00 csys = 0.12 CPU)
```

The advantage of writing a test in this table-driven format is that you can add another assertion (test case) without writing any more code. If you append another test case to the `%tests` hash as follows:

```
my %tests = (
  # me @ example.com
  'jrockway!~jrockway@example.com' => ['jrockway', 'jrockway',
    'example.com'],
  'another!~test@some-place.com' =>
  ['another', 'test', 'some-place.com'],
);
```

then you'll see two tests running:

```
$ prove -Ilib t/irc-parser-nickname.t t/irc-parser-nickname....ok
All tests successful.
Files=1, Tests=2, 0 wallclock secs ( 0.07 cusr + 0.01 csys = 0.08 CPU)
```

You can take this technique a step further and write test cases in a separate (non-Perl) file and load that file as the `%tests` hash. Then, you can have someone other than a programmer to write your test cases. If you choose to follow this route, then you should take a look at FIT (http://fit.c2.com/), and the `Test::FITesque` module on CPAN.

Testing a database

ChatStat is a pretty database-heavy application, so there's no way to avoid testing the database part. We can make testing the database less painful by providing an easy way for creating an empty database just for testing. This is easy to do with SQLite; we just create a temporary database, deploy our schema to it, run the tests, and then delete the database. Whenever I start a database application, I create a small module to automate this. For ChatStat, it's called `ChatStat::Test::Database`, and looks like the following:

```
package ChatStat::Test::Database;
use strict;
use warnings;
use Directory::Scratch;
use base 'ChatStat::Schema';
```

```
sub connect {
  my $class = shift;
  # setup temp space
  my $tmp = Directory::Scratch->new;
  my $db = $tmp->touch('database');
  # "connect" to temp database; deploy schema
  my $schema = $class->SUPER::connect("DBI:SQLite:$db");
  $schema->deploy;
  # done!
  return $schema;
}
```

All we do here is subclass our real DBIx::Class schema, and change the connect method to create a temporary database first. The Directory::Scratch module handles the management of the temporary scratch space, so we don't need to worry about cleaning up when we're done with tests.

Now we're ready to write database tests. The simplest thing to test would be the everything resultset, which will take "opinion" records and coalesce them into a ranked list of "things" with their point values. For example, given the input "test++, test--, foo++, foo++, bar--, and baz+-", we should get output like "foo => 2, baz => 0, test => 0, bar => -1".

Now that we know what we're testing (and have some sample data), we just need to have the computer check it for us. Let's create t/schema-report-everything.t as follows:

```
use strict;
use warnings;
use Test::More tests => 1;
use ChatStat::Test::Database;
use ChatStat::Robot::Action;
my @RECORDS = ([qw/test 1/],
   [qw/test -1/],
   [qw/foo   1/],
   [qw/foo   1/],
   [qw/bar -1/],
   [qw/baz   0/],
);
my @EXPECT = ([qw/foo   2/],
              [qw/baz   0/],
              [qw/test 0/],
              [qw/bar -1/],
);
```

```
my $schema = ChatStat::Test::Database->connect;
$schema->record(ChatStat::Robot::Action->
new({ who =>'foo!~foo@test.com',
      word => $_->[0],
      points => $_->[1],
      channel => '#test',
      reason => 'test',
      message => 'test',
}))
for @RECORDS;
my @everything = map {[ $_->thing, $_->total_points ]}
$schema->resultset('Things')->all;
is_deeply [sort {$a->[0] cmp $b->[0]} @everything],
[sort {$a->[0] cmp $b->[0]} @EXPECT],
'got expected everything';
```

With the database abstracted away, writing this test is easy. We start by defining our input data and output data. Then we connect to the database and add the input data to the database via `ChatStat::Robot::Action`. Then we run our `everything` report and see that it matches the expected data.

This is all that there is to testing. There are some other tests for other reports in ChatStat included with the book's source code, but they're not much different than the test we just saw. They simply add data to the database, and see if the results of queries make sense.

If all this is too complicated for you and if you are just beginning to test, you may want to simply start with `Test::Simple`. For more information on `Test::Simple`, refer to the following site:

```
http://search.cpan.org/~mschwern/Test-Simple-0.94/lib/Test/Simple.pm
```

If you would like to test the total number of tests executed, you can make use of the more evolved features of `Test::More` such as `done_testing`. For more information on `Test::More`, refer to the following site:

```
http://search.cpan.org/~mschwern/Test-Simple-0.94/lib/Test/More.pm
```

Once you are familiar with `Test::More`, you may also want to explore other modules such as `Test::Most` to begin with. Refer to the following site:

```
http://search.cpan.org/~ovid/Test-Most-0.21/lib/Test/Most.pm
```

Testing the web interface

Once you're confident that the backend is well tested, you need to make sure that the Catalyst part of your application is working smoothly. We have some more tools at our disposal for this task, Catalyst::Test and Test::WWW::Mechanize::Catalyst.

The basic idea here is to use Catalyst::Test (or similar) to make requests against the application and then see if the response contains the data we're looking for. (You can also do other things, like test if the HTML is valid and so on.)

As we still need the database, we'll have to jump through a few hoops to get a real Catalyst application to use the temporary database. What we need to do is create the testing database and then create a Catalyst config file that tells Catalyst to use the test database instead of the real one.

Here's the code for a module which does that, Chatstat::Test::Database::Live:

```
package ChatStat::Test::Database::Live;
use strict;
use warnings;
use ChatStat::Schema; use Directory::Scratch; use YAML qw(DumpFile);
use FindBin qw($Bin);
use base 'Exporter';
our @EXPORT = qw/schema/;
my $schema; my $config;
BEGIN {
  my $tmp = Directory::Scratch->new;
  my $dsn = "DBI:SQLite:$db";
  $schema = ChatStat::Schema->connect($dsn);
  $schema->deploy;
  $config = "$Bin/../chatstat_local.yml";
  DumpFile($config, {'Model::DBIC' => {connect_info => [$dsn]}});
}
sub schema { $schema };
END { unlink $config };
```

When you use this module, it will create a test database, connect to it, and write a "local" config file, with the connection information pointing to the test database. After this module is loaded and Catalyst is started, it will see the config file with the suffix _local and override the existing config file with the data contained in the local file. The END{} block will delete the local config file when the test is done running, so you won't have to worry about the local configuration cluttering up your disk.

Now that we have a test database shared between the test script and the Catalyst application, we can start writing some tests. Let's test the page at /things, which lists everything that has an entry in the database.

We'll start by creating the basic test file called t/app-live-everything.t as follows:

```
use strict;
use warnings;
use Test::More tests => 3;
use ChatStat::Robot::Action;
use ChatStat::Test::Database::Live;
use Test::WWW::Mechanize::Catalyst qw/ChatStat/;
my $schema = schema();
my $mech = Test::WWW::Mechanize::Catalyst->new;
# test empty page
is_deeply [$schema->resultset('Things')->everything], [], 'no things
yet';
$mech->get_ok('http://localhost/things/');
$mech->content_unlike(qr/test/);
```

This will create the database, and then use Test::WWW::Mechanize::Catalyst to start an instance of the application. Then we get the test database and a Test::WWW::Mechanize object (that runs requests against our application instead of the Internet).

With the setup done, we make sure there are no things in the database yet, and that they don't show up on the page. The $mech->get_ok method will run the /things/ action in our application (the localhost in the URL means "our application" in this case, not the web server running on the localhost). The $mech->content_unlike looks for a regex on the page, and is a passing test if the regex doesn't match. In this case, we're looking to ensure that the word "test" doesn't show up on the page yet. We'll add it to the page right before the next test; this is just a sanity check to make sure it doesn't show up there for some other reason.

Now, let's add test++ to the database, and see if the page updates correctly. First, let's add a little utility to make inserting test++ into the database easy:

```
sub add_opinion {
  $schema->record(ChatStat::Robot::Action->
    new({ who =>'foo!~foo@test.com',
      word => $_[0],
      points => $_[1],
      channel => '#test',
      reason => 'test',
      message => 'test',
    })
  );
}
```

I add this to the very bottom of the test file so that I don't have to skip past it when reading the tests.

After the existing tests, add the following:

```
# add an opinion add_opinion(test => 1);
my @things = $schema->resultset('Things')->everything->all;
is $things[0]->total_points, 1, 'got 1 point';
is $things[0]->thing, 'test', 'for test';
$mech->get_ok('http://localhost/things/');
$mech->content_like(qr/test/);
$mech->content_like(qr/1/);
```

Be sure to change the `test` counter at the top of the test to `8`, as we just added five more assertions.

These test cases look like the ones we saw previously. We add a piece of data to the database, check that it's in the resultset, and then see if the correct text appears on the web page. To complete this test, let's add some negative and zero entries, and make sure those work:

```
add_opinion(foo => 0);
$mech->get_ok('http://localhost/things/');
$mech->content_like(qr/foo/, 'foo shows up, even though it has 0
points');
add_opinion(test => -1);
add_opinion(test => -1);
$mech->get_ok('http://localhost/things/');
$mech->content_like(qr/negative/, q{now there's a negative entry});
$mech->content_unlike(qr/positive/, q{but no more positives});
add_opinion(bar => 1);
$mech->get_ok('http://localhost/things/');
$mech->content_like(qr/positive/, q{positive is back});
$mech->content_like(qr/bar/, q{and bar shows up});
```

That's all we need for this test. After running this, you can be pretty sure that adding opinions to the database is reflected in the web interface.

You can do many more things with `Test::WWW::Mechanize::Catalyst`. If you're looking for documentation, be sure to see the docs for `Test::WWW::Mechanize`, `WWW::Mechanize`, and `LWP::UserAgent`, as that's the inheritance hierarchy for `Test::WWW::Mechanize::Catalyst`. Anything that those modules can do, `Test::WWW::Mechanize::Catalyst` can do against your Catalyst application.

Testing the AddressBook

Testing the address book requires some techniques that we didn't need for ChatStat.
Most of the AddressBook is hidden behind a login screen, so we'll have to log in
for testing the application. It also requires us to fill out a lot of forms. Finally, it has
a JavaScript interface that we can't test without a live web browser. In this section,
we'll see how to test those parts of the application.

Logging in

We'll start by adding a test database module to AddressBook. This is almost an
exact copy of the one we created for ChatStat, but we add a convenience function
for creating a test user and logging in as that user:

```
package AddressBook::Test::Database::Live;
use strict;
use warnings;
use AddressBook::Schema::AddressDB;
use Directory::Scratch;
use YAML qw(DumpFile); use FindBin qw($Bin);
use base 'Exporter';
our @EXPORT = qw/log_in schema/;
my $schema;
my $config;
BEGIN {
  my $tmp = Directory::Scratch->new;
  my $db = $tmp->touch('db');
  my $dsn = "DBI:SQLite:$db";
  $schema = AddressBook::Schema::AddressDB->connect($dsn);
  $schema->deploy;
  $config = "$Bin/../addressbook_local.yml";
  DumpFile($config, {'Model::AddressDB' => {connect_info =>
    [$dsn]}});
}
sub schema { $schema };
sub log_in { # counts as 4 tests
my $mech = shift;
my $person = schema()->
resultset('People')->create({ firstname => 'Test',
                              lastname => 'User',
});
my $user = schema()->resultset('User')->
create({ username => 'test_user',
         password => 'ABCDEFGHI',
```

```
                person => $person,
    });
    $mech->get_ok('http://localhost/login');
    $mech->form_name('login');
    $mech->field(username => 'test_user');
    $mech->field(password => 'ABCDEFGHI');
    $mech->click('_submit');
    $mech->content_like(qr/Logged in successfully/);
    $mech->content_like(qr/Logged in as/);
    $mech->content_like(qr/Test User/);
    return $user;
}
END { unlink $config };
1;
```

The important part of this module is the `log_in` function. It creates a test user and uses Mechanize's form functionality to visit the login page. Enter the username and password, "click" submit and check that the user logged in successfully.

Now it's easy to start writing tests. Let's start by testing the login and logout functionality in a file called `t/live-login.t` as follows:

```
use strict;
use warnings;
use Test::More tests => 7;
use AddressBook::Test::Database::Live;
use Test::WWW::Mechanize::Catalyst 'AddressBook';
my $schema = schema();
my $mech = Test::WWW::Mechanize::Catalyst->new;
log_in($mech);
$mech->follow_link_ok({url_regex => qr/logout/},
    'follow logout link');
$mech->content_like(qr/Not logged in/);
$mech->content_unlike(qr/Test User/);
```

All we do here is create the schema and mech objects, try to log in (which is 4 assertions), and then try to log out. It's important to note that Mechanize is just like a regular web browser, and cookies and sessions are preserved. (There are even back, forward, and reload buttons that Mech can click.)

Testing forms

Now that we have a logged-in user, let's try creating a person, then adding an address for him. To get started, let's add the standard header to `t/live-add-person.t` as follows:

```
use strict;
use warnings;
use Test::More tests => 17;
use AddressBook::Test::Database::Live;
use Test::WWW::Mechanize::Catalyst 'AddressBook';
my $schema = schema();
my $mech = Test::WWW::Mechanize::Catalyst->new;
```

We'll continue by adding the user that `log_in` creates to the editor and viewer roles, so the ACL rules don't prevent the test from running:

```
# give user a role that lets him edit
my $user = log_in($mech); # 4 tests
my $viewer = $schema->resultset('Role')->create({ role => 'editor' });
my $editor = $schema->resultset('Role')->create({ role => 'viewer' });
$schema->resultset('UserRole')->create({ user => $user->id,
  role => $editor->id });
$schema->resultset('UserRole')->create({ user => $user->id,
  role => $viewer->id });
```

Now the test user can access and edit any part of the application. Let's try adding a new person by clicking links and filling out forms:

```
# now try adding a new person
$mech->get_ok('http://localhost/');
$mech->follow_link_ok({ text => 'Add a new person' });
$mech->content_like(qr/Adding a new person/, 'on the add person
  page');
$mech->form_number(1); # first form
$mech->field(firstname => 'Avery');
$mech->field(lastname  => 'Newperson');
$mech->click('_submit');
$mech->content_like(qr/Added Avery Newperson/, 'added a very new
  person');
```

Now there should be a new person, `Avery Newperson`, in the database. Let's retrieve a person record from the database to make sure that the interface is actually updating the database:

```
# find ID of new person
my $person = $schema->resultset('People')->
find(qw/Avery Newperson/, { key => 'name' });
my $id = $person->id;
ok $person->id > 0, 'got a person';
```

Now that we have the ID, let's add a home address for Avery:

```
# add an address
$mech->get_ok("http://localhost/address/add/$id");
$mech->content_like(qr/Adding a new address \s* for Avery
  Newperson/);
$mech->form_number(1);
$mech->field(location => 'Home');
$mech->field(postal => 'This is the postal address.');
$mech->field(phone => '123-456-7890');
$mech->field(email => 'test@example.com');
$mech->click('_submit');
$mech->content_like(qr/Added new address for Avery Newperson/);
$mech->content_like(qr/This is the postal address[.]/);
```

If that worked, the `$person` above should now have some related addresses as follows:

```
# see if that's in the database
my $address = $person->search_related('addresses')->first;
is $address->postal, 'This is the postal address.';
my $aid = $address->id;
```

Let's conclude by deleting the address as follows:

```
# now delete the address
$mech->follow_link_ok({url_regex => qr{address/delete/$aid} },
'blow away address');
$mech->content_like(qr/Deleted Avery Newperson's Home address/);
$mech->content_unlike(qr/This is the postal address[.]/);
```

Now you can run the test with `make test` or `prove`:

```
$ prove -Ilib t/live-add-person.t t/live-add-person....ok

All tests successful.

Files=1, Tests=17, 2 wallclock secs ( 1.68 cusr + 0.08 csys = 1.76
  CPU)
```

What used to be clicking through the interface manually is now an automatic test that can tell you in just a few seconds whether your application works. For a real application, you'll want to test everything, but this test is a good start.

Good tests will not only include tests of common cases but also edge cases. For example, if a field requires a number, what happens if the user enters "0 but true" (not a number) or "0e0" (a number)? Edge cases are where bugs show up, so try to be tricky and eliminate them in development. It's much more fun to fix a bug that a test finds as opposed to one that causes your site to go down at three in the morning.

As an aside, if you'd like to have your tests written automatically, you can install a CPAN module called `HTTP::Recorder`. `HTTP::Recorder` will act as a proxy between your application and the browser, and will translate any clicks and form submissions into code that you can paste into your Mechanize-based test. It's good for recording activity during user testing. If someone runs into a bug, you'll have a detailed log of what they clicked. You can copy that into your test file, add some assertions and you'll be able to fix the bug without having the user click through the interface to find the bug again.

Testing JavaScript

The remaining part of the AddressBook to be tested is the jemplate-based in-place address editor. To test this, we'll use a tool called **Selenium RC** (`http://www.openqa.org/`) to run tests directly in the browser. Selenium is a tool that sits between your application, the test script, and the web browser. The test script sends the Selenium server commands to run inside the web browser. The web browser then executes those commands, and returns the results to the Selenium server and then your test script.

It can be hard to get it up and running because it requires the **Java Runtime Environment** (JRE) and a working web browser. It is somewhat experimental, and the author has only tested on Cygwin with Firefox and IE and Debian GNU/Linux with Firefox.

Developing Selenium tests is pretty easy, thanks to the Selenium IDE Firefox extension available at `http://www.openqa.org/selenium-ide/`. It turns Firefox into an IDE that can record and edit tests, and save them to the Perl format.

To create a test against the Catalyst application, we'll start by recording the basic outline of the test with Selenium IDE.

To get started, start the AddressBook application, then open the IDE, and click the red record button. Then enter `http://localhost:3000/` in the address bar and wait for the page to load. Log in as the test user, navigate to the list of all addresses, click the first edit link to edit the address in place, and then change each of the fields to a new value. Click on **Submit** to store the changes, and then highlight all the text you just entered (now as part of the static page). Then, right-click and select **verifyTextPresent** for each field, as shown in the next screenshot:

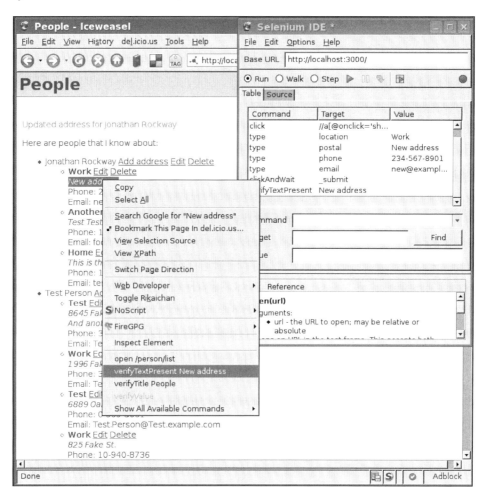

You should now have a Selenium test that appears as shown in the following screenshot:

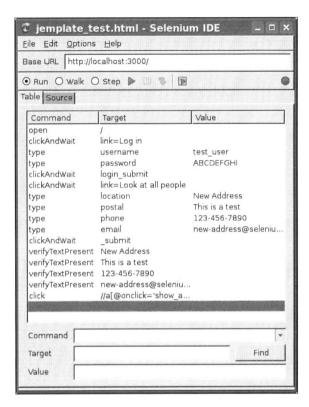

Now you can select all the records, change the clipboard format to Perl, and copy-and-paste the result into `t/selenium-edit.t`. We're going to edit the result a bit, though.

Here's what you get right out of the Selenium IDE:

```perl
$sel->open_ok("/");
$sel->click_ok("link=Log in");
$sel->wait_for_page_to_load_ok("30000");
$sel->type_ok("username", "test_user");
$sel->type_ok("password", "ABCDEFGHI");
$sel->click_ok("login_submit");
$sel->wait_for_page_to_load_ok("30000");
$sel->click_ok("link=Look at all people");
$sel->wait_for_page_to_load_ok("30000");
$sel->type_ok("location", "New Address");
```

```
$sel->type_ok("postal", "This is a test");
$sel->type_ok("phone", "123-456-7890");
$sel->type_ok("email", "new-address\@selenium.example.com");
$sel->click_ok("_submit");
$sel->wait_for_page_to_load_ok("30000");
$sel->is_text_present_ok("New Address");
$sel->is_text_present_ok("This is a test");
$sel->is_text_present_ok("123-456-7890");
$sel->is_text_present_ok("new-address\@selenium.example.com");
$sel->click_ok("//a[\@onclick='show_address_edit_form(6);return
   false;']");
```

To make this test run exactly as in the IDE, you just need to use `Test::WWW::Selenium::Catalyst` by adding something like the following code to the top of the file:

```
use strict;
use warnings;
use Test::More tests => 20;
use AddressBook::Test::Database::Live;
use Test::WWW::Selenium::Catalyst 'AddressBook';
my $sel = Test::WWW::Selenium::Catalyst->start;
```

There are still a few tweaks that we need to make the test work. We need to replace the hard-coded 6 with the ID of a sample address we create. We'll start by creating the necessary database records right before we create the `$sel` object:

```
my $person = schema()->
resultset('People')->create({ firstname => 'Test',
                              lastname => 'User',
 });
my $user = schema()->resultset('User')->
create({ username => 'test_user',
         password => 'ABCDEFGHI',
         person => $person,
});
my $address = schema()->resultset('Addresses')->
create({ person => $person->id,
  location => 'Home',
  postal => 'Postal address.',
  phone => 'Phone',
  email => 'email@email.com',
});
my $aid = $address->id;
```

Then you just need to replace the 6 on the last line with $aid. As soon as you do that, you should be able to run the test from prove. A web browser window will pop up and run the actions that your test script dictates. If everything goes well, you should see the "All tests successful" message at the very end. After it's working, you should add some more tests to see that the database was modified as you expected it to be.

If all doesn't go well, take a look at the manual page for Test::WWW::Selenium::Catalyst.

Once it's up and running you should find it a valuable testing tool, especially as the Selenium IDE makes it easy for anyone to record test cases.

Selenium isn't the only way to test JavaScript. You can also write Test::More style tests in JavaScript by using the Test::Simple module from the JSAN (the JavaScript version of the CPAN). Check it out at http://openjsan.org/doc/t/th/theory/Test/Simple/0.21/.

Summary

In this chapter, we learned how to write programs to test our Catalyst application automatically. We saw how to test the individual non-Catalyst components, and then saw how to test the components inside Catalyst with Test::WWW::Mechanize::Catalyst. We then learned how to test form-heavy applications with Mechanize. Finally, we learned how to test the JavaScript components with Selenium. Testing was once a tedious manual chore, but now the computer can do it for you!

Index

Symbols

A

address book application, testing
  about 211
  forms, testing 213-215
  JavaScript, testing 215-219
  logging in 211, 212
address objects 163
after method 182
AJAX
  about 165
  implementing 168-173
all_things method 132
Apache, web server
  about 193
  FastCGI 193, 194
  mod_perl 195
  mod_perl, Catalyst application serving 196
  mod_perl, performance enhancing 196
  static content 194
API (Application Programming Interface) 155
API key 158
application
  deploying 189, 190
Args. CaptureArgs 138
asynchronous JavaScript and XML. *See* AJAX
authentication
  about 87
  application, configuring 96
  guts, implementing 96
  schema files, creating 92-95
  tables, creating in database 91
Authentication::Store::Htpasswd 88
authorization
  generate_reports() command 89
  plugin 89
Authorization::Roles, authorization plugin 89

B

begin method 158
belongs_to relationship 95 , 109
Blog::Backend::Filesystem object 153
Blog::Model::Filesystem::Post class 152
BUILD method 180

C

cancel_address_edit function 171
CaptureArgs 138
Catalyst
  address book application, testing 211
  application, deploying 189-191
  application architecture 8
  application skeleton, creating 17-20
  ChatStat application 103
  ChatStat application, testing 204, 205
  CPAN modules, installing 41
  components 10
  configuration management 192
  flexibility 10
  help 13, 14
  helper scripts 23
  installation, testing 13
  installing 11
  installing, from CPAN 12
  installing, via operating system's package manager 11
  mechanics 202, 203
  Model 9
  model, creating 43
  Moose 10
  outside components, using 75-79
  PAR, deploying 191
  reliability 11
  reusability 10
  URL requests, handling 26-28
  View 9
  View, adding 28-31
  web server, configuring 192
Catalyst::Controller::REST 157
Catalyst::Model::DBI 141
Catalyst::Model::Factory::PerRequest module 153
Catalyst::Plugin::Authentication 87
Catalyst::Plugin::Cache::Store::FastMmap 167
Catalyst::Plugin::ConfigLoader::Environment extension 192
Catalyst::Plugin::Session::Store:: FastMmap 70
Catalyst::Test 208
Catalyst::View::Jemplate 166

Thank you for buying
Catalyst 5.8

About Packt Publishing

Packt, pronounced 'packed', published its first book "*Mastering phpMyAdmin for Effective MySQL Management*" in April 2004 and subsequently continued to specialize in publishing highly focused books on specific technologies and solutions.

Our books and publications share the experiences of your fellow IT professionals in adapting and customizing today's systems, applications, and frameworks. Our solution based books give you the knowledge and power to customize the software and technologies you're using to get the job done. Packt books are more specific and less general than the IT books you have seen in the past. Our unique business model allows us to bring you more focused information, giving you more of what you need to know, and less of what you don't.

Packt is a modern, yet unique publishing company, which focuses on producing quality, cutting-edge books for communities of developers, administrators, and newbies alike. For more information, please visit our website: www.packtpub.com.

About Packt Open Source

In 2010, Packt launched two new brands, Packt Open Source and Packt Enterprise, in order to continue its focus on specialization. This book is part of the Packt Open Source brand, home to books published on software built around Open Source licences, and offering information to anybody from advanced developers to budding web designers. The Open Source brand also runs Packt's Open Source Royalty Scheme, by which Packt gives a royalty to each Open Source project about whose software a book is sold.

Writing for Packt

We welcome all inquiries from people who are interested in authoring. Book proposals should be sent to author@packtpub.com. If your book idea is still at an early stage and you would like to discuss it first before writing a formal book proposal, contact us; one of our commissioning editors will get in touch with you.

We're not just looking for published authors; if you have strong technical skills but no writing experience, our experienced editors can help you develop a writing career, or simply get some additional reward for your expertise.

Zend Framework 1.8 Web Application Development

ISBN: 978-1-847194-22-0   Paperback: 380 pages

Design, develop, and deploy feature-rich PHP web applications with this MVC framework

1. Create powerful web applications by leveraging the power of this Model-View-Controller-based framework

2. Learn by doing – create a "real-life" storefront application

3. Covers access control, performance optimization, and testing

4. Best practices, as well as debugging and designing discussion

PHP 5 CMS Framework Development

ISBN: 978-1-847193-57-5   Paperback: 348 pages

Expert insight and practical guidance to creating an efficient, flexible, and robust framework for a PHP 5-based content management system

1. Learn how to design, build, and implement a complete CMS framework for your custom requirements

2. Implement a solid architecture with object orientation, MVC

3. Build an infrastructure for custom menus, modules, components, sessions, user tracking, and more

4. Written by a seasoned developer of CMS applications

Please check **www.PacktPub.com** for information on our titles

Expert PHP 5 Tools

ISBN: 978-1-847198-38-9   Paperback: 468 pages

Proven enterprise development tools and best practices for designing, coding, testing, and deploying PHP applications

1. Best practices for designing, coding, testing, and deploying PHP applications – all the information in one book

2. Learn to write unit tests and practice test-driven development from an expert

3. Set up a professional development environment with integrated debugging capabilities

4. Develop your own coding standard and enforce it automatically

CodeIgniter for Rapid PHP Application Development

ISBN: 978-1-847191-74-8   Paperback: 260 pages

Improve your PHP coding productivity with the free compact open-source MVC CodeIgniter framework!

1. Clear, structured tutorial on working with CodeIgniter

2. Careful explanation of the basic concepts of CodeIgniter and its MVC architecture

3. Using CodeIgniter with databases, HTML forms, files, images, sessions, and email

4. Building a dynamic website quickly and easily using CodeIgniter's prepared code

Please check **www.PacktPub.com** for information on our titles

CodeIgniter 1.7

ISBN: 978-1-847199-48-5   Paperback: 300 pages

Improve your PHP coding productivity with the free compact open-source MVC CodeIgniter framework!

1. Clear, structured tutorial on working with CodeIgniter for rapid PHP application development

2. Careful explanation of the basic concepts of CodeIgniter and its MVC architecture

3. Use CodeIgniter with databases, HTML forms, files, images, sessions, and email

4. Full of ideas and examples with instructions making it ideal for beginners to CodeIgniter

CakePHP Application Development

ISBN: 978-1-847193-89-6   Paperback: 332 pages

Step-by-step introduction to rapid web development using the open-source MVC CakePHP framework

1. Develop cutting-edge Web 2.0 applications, and write PHP code in a faster, more productive way

2. Walk through the creation of a complete CakePHP Web application

3. Customize the look and feel of applications using CakePHP layouts and views

Please check **www.PacktPub.com** for information on our titles

Smarty PHP Template Programming and Applications

ISBN: 978-1-904811-40-4   Paperback: 256 pages

A step-by-step guide to building PHP web sites and applications using the Smarty templating engine

1. Bring the benefits of Smarty to your PHP programming

2. Give your designers the power to modify content and layout without PHP programming

3. Produce code that is easier to debug, maintain, and modify

4. Useful for both Smarty developers and users

Symfony 1.3 Web Application Development

ISBN: 978-1-84719-456-5   Paperback: 228 pages

Design, develop, and deploy feature-rich, high-performance PHP web applications using the Symfony framework

1. Create powerful web applications by leveraging the power of this Model-View-Controller-based framework

2. Covers all the new features of version 1.3 – many exciting plug-ins for you

3. Learn by doing without getting into too much theoretical detail – create a "real-life" milkshake store application

4. Includes best practices to shorten your development time and improve performance

Please check **www.PacktPub.com** for information on our titles

1108642R0

Printed in Great Britain by
Amazon.co.uk, Ltd.,
Marston Gate.